EMPOWERED BY FAITH

EMPOWERED BY FAITH

EXPERIENCING GOD'S LOVE EVERY DAY

RICHARD G. CAPEN JR.

ZONDERVAN®

GRAND RAPIDS, MICHIGAN 49530 USA

ZONDERVAN.COM/
AUTHOR**TRACKER**

Empowered by Faith
Copyright © 2006 by Richard G. Capen Jr.

Requests for information should be addressed to:
Zondervan, *Grand Rapids, Michigan 49530*

Library of Congress Cataloging-in-Publication Data

Capen, Richard G.
    Empowered by faith : experiencing God's love every day /
Richard G. Capen, Jr.—1st ed.
    p. cm.
    Includes index.
    ISBN-13: 978-0-310-26950-2
    ISBN-10: 0-310-26950-4
    1. Christian life. I. Title.
BV4501.3.C366   2006
248.4—dc22

    2006010169

This edition printed on acid-free paper.

Interior design by Beth Shagene

Printed in the United States of America

06 07 08 09 10 11 12 • 18 17 16 15 14 13 12 11 10 9 8 7 6 5 4 3 2 1

IN APPRECIATION

After all our hopes and dreams have come and gone
And our children sift through all we've left behind,
May the clues that they discover and the memories they uncover
Become the light that leads them to the road we each must find.

Let us leave to those behind us the heritage of faithfulness
Passed on through godly lives.

Oh, may all who come behind us find us faithful....

—Jon Mohr

TO JOAN

For more than forty-four years Joan has been my inseparable partner and mother of our three children. She empowers me every day. She radiates God's love and grace with every life she touches. There is no way to describe adequately the love and respect I have for her.

Years before we met, I prayed that God would bring into my life someone who could nurture my faith, build a close family, and share a life of love, service, and adventure. Through His abundant grace, my prayers were answered far beyond my wildest dreams. For that gift I am enormously blessed, knowing that, through the sacrifice and promise of His Son, Joan and I are united for all eternity.

TO OUR FAMILY

We thank God for our most important blessings and legacy: our son, Chris Capen; our daughter Kelly Douglas and her husband, JD; and our daughter Carrie Hasler and her husband, James. We are so grateful for what they are doing to honor and empower us beyond measure.

And we praise God for the precious gift of grandchildren: Courtney Douglas, Collin Douglas, and Cate Hasler. And as this book goes to press, Cate has a little brother or sister on the way. They, in unique and wonderful ways, are bringing us such great pride and fulfillment with their special energy, endless enthusiasm, and almost insatiable curiosity about life. Each continues to enrich our lives in many, many ways.

CONTENTS

This book seeks to help us put God's empowering love on the front page of life. Here we discover some of the basic ingredients that will lead us to a more fulfilling purpose—one centered on God's love, compassion, and hope.

It is essential that we put our lives in God's hands, comforted by the reality that He leads the way. We need to have faith that when we put ourselves in His hands, He will lead us on an amazing adventure that will give us a life we never dreamed possible.

Finding ultimate meaning in life takes commitment and determination—at work, at church, in our neighborhoods, at school, with friends—wherever we might be. This is the makeover we really need.

God wants to do many wonderful things in our lives. All will require change along the way. Change is good for the soul. It helps us sort out what's truly important in our lives—now and in the future.

FOREWORD

This book needed to be written, and Dick Capen was the man to write it.

Dick Capen is one of the most gifted men I have ever had the pleasure of knowing: dedicated public servant, outstanding newspaper publisher, effective diplomat. As a committed Christian he also knows what it means to put his faith into action, not just one day out of the week but — as the subtitle of this challenging book declares — the other six days as well.

Drawing on a lifetime of wisdom and experience, he shares practical insights and principles that every Christian will find helpful, no matter who we are or what God has called us to do.

Dr. Billy Graham
Montreat, North Carolina

■ ■ ■

When Dick Capen told me he was writing a follow-up to his bestseller, *Finish Strong*, I couldn't imagine what he would do for an encore. I should have known that a man whose career has included high-profile stints as a publisher and a diplomat would still have plenty of wit and wisdom to share with the world.

Capen's choice of theme for this second book — rediscovering our faith in turbulent times — is certainly a fitting one. When I first met him in the 1980s, during his tenure as publisher of *The Miami Herald*, strident rhetoric and escalating violence between ethnic communities were threatening to pull Miami apart. When others might have battened down the hatches against growing unrest, Capen chose not merely to take the high road — instead, he strapped on racing shoes and sprinted to his goal: building bridges among warring factions. Anyone who spent time in Miami during that divisive period knows that his conviction, his commitment, and above all, his can-do attitude played critical roles in helping the city weather one of its darkest hours.

The benefits of the type of upbeat, optimistic thinking that Capen displayed at the *Herald* — and that he continues to culti-vate — should never be underestimated. I know from my own life that a positive outlook is the not-so-secret ingredient in handling anything from a heart attack to a grueling hundred-hour-a-week schedule to an economic downturn. It's often said that "you are what you eat." I believe people are also what they think. Naysay-ers who see only the negative side of things often fulfill their own prophecies. But if, as Capen has shown, you insist on finding the good in whatever life hands you, you will do more than just sur-vive — you will *thrive*.

J. W. "BILL" MARRIOTT JR.
Chairman and CEO, Marriott International

■ ■ ■

Dick Capen has excelled at everything he has undertaken — from his devoted family life to his valuable public service to our nation to his effective leadership in business and journalism. In all Dick's successes, he has been guided by a contagious sense of optimism and strong personal values that his friends like me have admired and tried to emulate.

In this book Dick explains how to instill the qualities of optimism, hope, and encouragement into our daily lives. I can't think of a better person to provide us with such valuable and timely insights. He explains how to look for the best in life and how to believe that almost anything is possible if we develop a positive attitude and work hard enough to achieve our goals. Dick Capen is a shining example of hope, optimism, and hard work. Those who read this book will have a new chance to follow Dick's guidance and example and become unabashed optimists.

FORMER U.S. SENATOR SAM NUNN
Georgia

▪ ▪ ▪

My friend Dick Capen has been empowered by his faith in every aspect of his life, from his time in public service to his successful career in the private sector. This book serves as a wonderful guide for all of us to likewise seek out God's love and put it into action every day of the week, every week of the year.

FRANKLIN GRAHAM
President and CEO, Billy Graham Evangelistic Association

▪ ▪ ▪

Out of the depth of life experience, my friend Dick Capen delivers "the goods" about life, faith, and the incredible love of God. I found myself liking what Dick wrote because it kept striking a reality chord in my heart. I trust his book will do that for you as well.

JOE STOWELL
Teaching Pastor, Harvest Bible Chapel, Illinois

▪ ▪ ▪

In a day when Christians are told to keep their faith to themselves, Dick Capen has written an important new book demonstrating that faith applies to all of life. Dick Capen is an inspiration to me as he has been to millions of other people. May God use this new book to help strengthen Christians in their daily walk.

D. JAMES KENNEDY
Senior Minister, Coral Ridge Presbyterian Church, Florida

■ ■ ■

A day with Dick Capen is a time to treasure. And in print he is just as authentic as in person. If you are looking for authenticity, counsel, and encouragement that you can trust, consider Capen.

DAN YEARY
Senior Pastor, North Phoenix Baptist Church, Arizona

■ ■ ■

Dick Capen has hit a home run. *Empowered by Faith* will be of inestimable value to each of us as we cope with the new and unusual challenges of the twenty-first century.

GENERAL P. X. KELLEY
28th Commandant of the U.S. Marine Corps

■ ■ ■

Dick Capen worked with me in the Department of Defense on the important problems of our POWs and MIAs. He was a great help to the families of these servicemen. His faith and love of God was a great inspiration to all of us.

MELVIN R. LAIRD
Former Secretary of Defense

INTRODUCTION

GOD'S PROVIDENCE

The world is ripe and ready, I believe, for men and women who recognize that they are not immune from the predicaments of the day ... and who are ready to see that the providence of God may have brought them to such a time as this.

U.S. Senator Elizabeth Dole, North Carolina

REBUILDING

We've always needed God from the very beginning of this nation, but today we need Him especially.... Now we have a choice: whether to implode and disintegrate emotionally and spiritually as a people and a nation — or whether we choose to become stronger through all of this struggle — to rebuild a solid foundation. I believe we are in the process of starting to rebuild on that foundation.

Dr. Billy Graham, at the observance of the National Day of Prayer and Remembrance, September 14, 2001

HIS PURPOSE

We are not this story's author, who fills time and eternity with His purpose. Yet His purpose is achieved in our duty.

President George W. Bush, inaugural address, January 2001

I am writing this book because I am an optimist, and I believe all Christians ought to be optimists too. What an amazing time to be alive, and what a defining time to share what we believe!

All around us are people who are frightened and angry over terrorism, worried about the economy, and fed up with politics, yet searching for something real and authentic that will help them cope with the new reality. They hunger to know God's purpose for them and for their loved ones. That's why we who are followers of Christ are at a unique juncture in human history and must capture the potential of this moment.

That's what being *Empowered by Faith* is all about: how we can fully experience God's love — and successfully share it too.

When we put our trust in God, we are empowered with His love, compassion, and hope. Through Him we discover a unique purpose for life and the strength to use His gifts to serve others. This is because our loving Lord not only helps us overcome weakness, failure, and tragedy, but also wants us to experience the joy that comes through an outward focus on the needs of others.

This book is about how you can tap that empowerment and use it in all aspects of your life, every day. Through God's enabling love you will find yourself strengthened — in fact, compelled — to discover how He wants to use you to radiate His purpose for you.

ON THE RECORD

Created for a Purpose

We are created with a capacity to have a personal relationship with God. If you believe you evolved, you say your life is an accident, maybe even a mistake. You have come from nowhere. You are going nowhere and your life has no eternal purpose.

Evangelist Anne Graham Lotz

God is the Almighty, the Powerful One, the Comforter, the Creator of "all things bright and beautiful." Through His love you can find hope when you have given up. You can discover strength when you are weak and success when you have stumbled.

This book springs from my desire to help you put God's empowering love on the front page of your life, just as others have helped me to do. Here you will discover some of the basic ingredients that will lead you to a more fulfilling purpose — one centered on God's love, compassion, and hope.

The message of *Empowered by Faith* is one of encouragement as you seek to live out your faith and share God's many blessings with your family, friends, and others who touch your life along the way. Here I hope you will find practical ways to radiate your faith to those you care most about, not just on Sundays but throughout the week. And I am the first to admit that this is no easy task in a contemporary world almost obsessed with secularism and overwhelmed with tragedy, uncertainty, and global crisis.

ON THE RECORD

Children of God

Do everything without complaining or arguing, so that you may become blameless and pure, children of God without fault in a crooked and depraved generation, in which you shine like stars.

Philippians 2:14 – 15

God strengthens us with His overwhelming love and, with that gift, provides each of us with the ability and responsibility to share His grace and assurance with those around us. However, to accept God's empowerment we must first surrender our own sense of control and power. When life delivers a crisis or tragedy, we too often believe we can solve problems on our own — but we can't. It is only by turning to God for help — "surrendering all," as the hymn goes — that we can receive His empowerment.

My careers in newspaper publishing and public service have spanned more than forty years. At every turn, through every crisis, I tried to remember that my own life is guided by a loving God who has given me the energy, experience, and balance to live my life fully, to lead with compassion, and to uplift those who help make the world a better place.

While my professional life has included extended service in the military and public service, the longest span of my career placed me in key roles at Knight Ridder, Inc., highlighted by eight years at the helm of one of America's great daily newspapers: *The Miami Herald.* At the time, Knight Ridder was one of the nation's largest publicly held media companies, with newspapers in more than forty cities across America.

During my years in South Florida I loved everything about the process of delivering the news to a large, diverse, metropolitan community (in reality an international city).

— The smell of ink and newsprint when you walked into the pressroom, where eleven lines of huge, two-story presses spanned more than a city block.
— The skepticism of the veteran editors, the idealism of the young reporters.
— The daily opportunities to help shape public opinion, especially on important local issues.

At times we needed the wisdom of Solomon to help define the balance of our newspaper in a region uplifted by potential as an international city and, at the same time, ravaged by division, natural disasters, and drugs. All this 24 hours a day, 365 days a year.

While my time at the newspaper was often dominated by controversy and bad news, I believed passionately that we needed to tell the stories of what was right in our community. No matter how tough things were, such good news helped keep our readers encouraged and full of hope.

— The quiet heroes who invested their lives in their neighborhoods.

— The entrepreneurs who created jobs for our citizens.
— The houses of worship that reached out to Protestants, Catholics, Jews, and all shades of denominations in between.
— New immigrants from the Caribbean and South America who provided some of the best examples of the American Dream.

Certainly we had a sacred responsibility to tell what I referred to as "hard truths" — those painful stories ranging from human tragedy to brutal crime, from the ravages of cocaine to scandals in local government, to ruthless abuses by brutal Latin American dictators, to the story about a U.S. senator's affair with a South Florida woman while campaigning for president in 1984. Our reporting was important and often controversial, but such are the perils of the business. What gave me the greatest sense of accomplishment, however, were those news and feature stories that showed the better side of life in ways that would uplift, not discourage, our readers.

I know what you're thinking: "The last thing we need is another Pollyanna telling us to just be nice and everything will be all right." You're right. The *last* thing we need are platitudes and simplistic solutions to the complex and even frightening problems we face today. And yet I have to be honest with you. The longer I live, and the more I reflect on the condition of our world, the more I am convinced that what you believe is more important than what you know. That character matters more than credentials. That those who claim to follow the teachings of Jesus have a wonderful opportunity to shine like stars and brighten the night we find ourselves in.

What does this mean for you? Does your faith in God radiate just on Sunday, or are you willing to share it during the week with friends, neighbors, and colleagues at work? These are not abstract subjects for another day when tough times come. As we have learned so dramatically, our lives and our country have been tested to the core in recent years. If you cannot articulate how essential a loving God is to you in such times, when can you step forward and share your faith?

I am still amazed — and I suspect you might be too — at the way people responded to the horrible tragedy of September 11, 2001. In an instant, the true soul of America was opened for the whole world to see. Politics and division no longer mattered. As a nation we were one — hurting yet hopeful, shaken but determined to prevail. We were terribly frightened and knew instinctively that our lives had changed forever.

I do not ever recall such an outpouring of love and faith in God as occurred in those weeks following the collapse of the World Trade Center. Ordinary citizens spoke openly about how they turned to prayer as followers of Jesus Christ. Passengers on those doomed planes were heard sharing the Lord's Prayer together with loved ones via their cell phones.

Busloads of volunteers headed for Ground Zero to help in any way they could. Restaurants in the area donated food to the firefighters and other rescue workers. Within days, homemade banners and posters appeared on the plywood barriers outlining the cavernous crater where the towers once stood. They were lovingly crafted in elementary schools, community centers, churches, and synagogues across the nation by people who wanted somehow to provide a healing message.

In the first weeks that followed this awful tragedy, prayer and other expressions of dependence on a loving God were not only acceptable, but cherished. Without embarrassment or hesitation, people all over the country spoke passionately about how their lives were being sustained by faith in God and through the power of prayer. There was a huge outpouring of America's soul. Our churches and synagogues were overflowing. We stopped in our tracks for prayer and quiet reflection.

Some who clearly had no faith were moved by the public prayers and messages of hope from our religious and political leaders. For a brief time, we as a nation turned to God, knowing that He would help us get through the crisis.

Wouldn't it be great if we could capture that spirit and make it a more consistent part of our lives — both as individuals and as a community? I am not talking about forcing people to believe, but somehow they simply cannot miss the meaning of life and the power of God's love when there is such an outpouring of the best of America. In recent years it seems that we have been hit by one huge crisis after another — 9/11, the wars in Afghanistan and Iraq, the devastating hurricanes in Florida and Louisiana and Mississippi, the catastrophic tsunami in South Asia, the overwhelming HIV/AIDS epidemic in Africa. Yet, over and over again millions of generous Americans are stepping forward to donate money, food, clothing, medical supplies, and thousands of hours of on-the-scene volunteer help.

ON THE RECORD

Trusting in Him

Every day I put my faith on the line. I have never seen God. In a world where nearly everything can be weighed, explained, quantified, subject to psychological analysis and scientific control, I persist in making the center of my life a God whom no one has seen, nor ear heard, whose will no one can probe.

Author Eugene Peterson

It is during times like these that there is an overwhelming belief in something greater than ourselves that brings our nation together. And I wonder today: why can't we keep this faith alive 24/7? Why can't we apply the same energy and creativity to the everyday problems we all face? Why can't the church be known as the one place you can always depend on for finding hope, joy, acceptance, and comfort? Why can't Christians be the people who stand out as beacons of hope and grace?

And here is the central point: God surely empowers us.

For many years as a public servant, newspaper publisher, and ambassador, I was reluctant to be open about my religious convictions. I didn't overtly try to hide the fact that I was a Christian, but at the same time I kept my beliefs pretty much to myself. It wasn't that I was ashamed of what I believed. It was more a case of being uncomfortable with the image that people of faith in the United States had developed. Mention "Christian" in the newsroom, and the distaste was almost palpable. Mean-spirited. Judgmental. Prejudiced. Boring. They don't even get along with each other. And to be truthful, I did not think those adjectives were unearned. Some of the Christians I knew fit that description.

I have since come to realize that there were a lot of Christians just like me who kept pretty quiet about their beliefs, especially on the job or in the marketplace. And maybe that's part of the problem. By default we have failed to stand up for all that is important to us.

Do you feel that way too? Do you ever wonder about that huge gap between those feelings you have on Sunday and those you have on the other six days of the week? Maybe your goal is simply to live out your faith in everyday ways, through simple personal example, but you need the courage to do so. Perhaps your priority is to draw people together rather than to divide or antagonize. If so, I trust that many of the quotes and stories in this book will give you fresh hope.

And, most important, if you have worried that you might offend others by discussing things spiritual, I trust that you will find new encouragement to acknowledge your faith in God.

This may seem like an unlikely guide for your own journey, so maybe a few words about my own spiritual story will put you at ease. I have had to ask myself whether my priority centers on my career and the comforts that come with it, or whether my life is focused on commitment to a higher purpose.

ON THE RECORD

God Is Calling You

Having a clear purpose makes it easier to accept God's gift of grace and continue to trust it. After all, if we talk about your "calling," we must also talk about the "caller."

Ken Blanchard
Author and management consultant,
in *We Are the Beloved*

These are tough questions for a guy who came up the hard way, and they may be tough for you as well. But they are the questions that matter — the ones that will help us get our priorities straight. For you see, as much as I love this country and enjoy the freedom and abundance it gives me, I had to come to a point in my own life — I was married and my wife and I had a young family — where I acknowledged that too many times I was more of a cultural Christian than a true believer for whom Jesus Christ was central.

I believe that the principle source of moral authority comes from God, not government, and that obedience to Him makes us better people than would otherwise be the case. But it's not about being better people as a way to earn favor with God. As a follower of the teachings of Jesus, my mission is to reflect His love to others. I firmly believe that if I do that, and if you do that, and if all of us who are Christians do that, we really can change the world!

After all, that is the Great Commission that Jesus commanded us to follow:

All authority in heaven and on earth has been given to me. Therefore go and make disciples of all nations ... (Matthew 28:18–19).

In order to meet today's challenges, we must not be shy about living our faith and quietly radiating its inspirational power for those around us to see. In a nutshell, this is the driving theme of this book: to encourage you to rediscover your inner faith and to share it effectively in a secular, too-often faithless world — not just on Sundays but throughout the entire week. Not in a sectarian, strong-armed manner, where having the "right" truth is more important than having the right spirit, but in a humble and eloquent reflection of the values that stem from our faith as Christians.

In this book we explore practices and traits that will help you rekindle your faith and character. And you will find some inspiring examples of God-loving people who embody the finest values of the American ideals. Here you will find useful, practical ideas for that renewal. You also will find inspiration from timeless Scripture to help you — in practical, everyday ways — live your faith in the mostly secular world around you.

Included are comments from some familiar names, and I trust you will be uplifted — as am I — by their underlying message of hope. Through them you will be reminded that you are not alone in a desire to reflect God's love every day, in every way. Some may even inspire you to even greater faithful service in the name of a loving God.

Now, let's get on with the task.

Dick Capen

ON THE RECORD

Included throughout this book are dozens of wonderful gems of wisdom from some people who have discovered the core of their inner spirit. Their lives, you will find, are supercharged with new excitement generated each step of the way. Their faith in God is alive and well. Their willingness to acknowledge Jesus Christ as their Savior is strong.

Their personal testimonies, along with relevant scriptural quotes, are labeled "On the Record" and are displayed and highlighted for easy reference.

As you read each thought, stop and reflect on what each person has to say, on what the Bible tells us. How can these thoughts help you? How have others shared their faith? How did they live it every day? Will it work in your life? When an idea strikes a chord, write it down, highlight it in the book, copy it for quick reference, and email it to friends. Stick it on your refrigerator door, the bathroom mirror, or your computer screen. Share it with loved ones.

FAITH KEEPERS

Each chapter concludes with a wrap-up feature, Faith Keepers. In it are useful, practical tips that can be used as a checklist, designed to help you discover, strengthen, and tune up your inner spirit. Above all, they are designed to empower you in His service.

Chapter 1

TRUST GOD

No Matter What

Be cheerful no matter what; pray all the time; thank God no matter what happens.

1 Thessalonians 5:16–18 *The Message*

The Bottom Line of Life

It is foolish to seek after honors, power, and wealth.... The most significant endeavor of the Christian is to constantly seek to become closer to Christ.... Whatever good I have done, and whatever talents I have had to accomplish that good, have been the gifts of the Almighty.

Judge Bill Hoeveler, Federal District Court, South Florida

Taking Control

I am totally convinced that the essential difference between one man and the next, one of whom becomes a man of achievement and distinction while the other remains one of the crowd, is the former's greater capacity to manage himself.... Beginning today, stop doing some one thing you know you should not do and start doing each day some one thing you know you should do....

Stay with it long enough and the world will be yours.

Author James Michener

It was an inevitable moment for a proud ninety-two-year-old lady who had recently lost her husband of seventy years. The time had arrived for her to move into a nursing home. Her caretaker, dreading the conversation, was trying to make the best of the situation by describing in glowing terms where she was headed as they drove across town to her tiny new room.

"I will love it," the lady said.

"How can that be?" her friend asked. "You haven't seen the room yet."

With that, the lady replied, "That doesn't have anything to do with it. Happiness is something you decide in advance."

Wow! What a spirit! Mrs. Jones was approaching what could have been an uncomfortable experience, but instead she chose to make it a brand-new adventure. What a wonderful way to go through life!

I believe people of faith must be people who radiate their faith no matter the circumstances. As we learn from Mrs. Jones, optimistic and hopeful people don't resist the changes that come along, but embrace them. Simply trust that God has a brand-new adventure for you to enjoy.

While I am a big proponent of making wise plans for the future, sometimes we can rely too much on our own wisdom and not enough on God's. In all likelihood, Mrs. Jones resisted moving out of her home for years but knew that when the moment of change arrived, her life was in the hands of the Lord.

It is important to put your trust in God, knowing that He leads the way especially when you face important decisions or major crises. As I have learned over the years — often the hard way — it is very difficult to let go and to let God be in charge, not on your timetable but on His.

One of the most important decisions in my life began with a long, lonely drive from Washington, D.C., to San Diego. I was unemployed and broke and had decided to head west, where I had been stationed in the Navy two years earlier. Like thousands before me, I had fallen in love with Southern California and was determined someday to return. This seemed like an ideal moment to make the big move. I was starting over again.

In June of that year I had quit a job with a Washington-area trade association and signed up to be part of then–Vice President Richard Nixon's 1960 presidential campaign staff. I had lived in the nation's capital, Dwight Eisenhower was a universally beloved and respected president, and many felt that his popularity would help the White House aspirations of Nixon. As often happens with people living in Washington, I had become hooked on politics and felt my candidate was sure to win. I wanted to be a part of the action.

For six months I traveled the country, helping the Nixon advance team plan campaign stops. If politics was addictive then, it was also fun. The crowds were huge, and each candidate worked hard to outdraw his opponent at every campaign stop. We soon learned we were up against a formidable, charismatic opponent in John F. Kennedy. By November the momentum had shifted from Nixon, and Kennedy won by a narrow margin. Richard Nixon

ON THE RECORD

Anything Is Possible

Don't allow people's negativity or discouragement to stop you from trying to realize your dreams. Anything is possible if you respect yourself and are willing to work hard.

Stacey Wing
Nashville, Tennessee

was history — or so we thought at that time. At a young age I had learned that there is no more lonely feeling than that experienced the morning after a losing campaign. The workers in the Nixon camp scattered.

I moved out of my Washington apartment, packed all my worldly possessions in the trunk of my almost new (but heavily financed) Ford convertible, and headed west. I thought my white car with red leather upholstery was perfect for the world of sun and beaches even if the bank owned it. I still had eighteen monthly payments to make, but why worry? I was moving to the Golden State, the land of perpetual summer. I had no job leads and knew only a handful of people in San Diego, and by the time I crossed the state line into California, my life's savings had shrunk to $75.

There was serious work to do, but how could I not be optimistic? A life full of wonderful options lay ahead. I had graduated from college, had completed my active duty commitment to the U.S. Navy, and had tasted the world of presidential politics. Single and twenty-six, I was riding high. Even though I had absolutely no tangible reason for believing so, I was going to win again. Little did I know that this was the beginning of a fantastic new chapter in life.

As I think back on similar moments of decision and change, I am struck by the sense that God's hand was behind each one. I cringe to think what might have happened at each point where a change was about to take place, if I had relied more on my own plans rather than follow what God had in store for me. Opportunities opened, not by chance but by His grace. I had prayed a lot about this change in my life, but the ultimate decisions I faced were made easier because I sensed that He was at my side.

You likewise have probably passed through life-changing thresholds and know the feeling. The process is a little scary. There may be many choices — perhaps too many — or maybe you worry that you are backed into a corner with few options. Sometimes you are totally alone and must move on. Whatever the circumstance, a moment of truth is fast approaching and you must choose your course. Conventional wisdom says you make a list of all the pros and cons, and I'm all for that. Unconventional wisdom says you lay it all before God and boldly walk through the doors He opens for you. That's usually the scary part, but it is a great way to live!

Of course, it's not quite that easy. You need to be really in tune with God and not just go through the motions. For me, it has always meant finding a quiet place to pray and seek His leading. I recall going to the Washington National Cathedral one Sunday and praying for God's guidance as I thought about moving west. I also remember, after a whirlwind series of dates with Joan, feeling that God had brought us together and that she should become my partner. I'm so glad I paid attention, as she has been by my side for almost forty-five years. But again, it was that strong sense that this was as much God's plan as mine.

Mount Soledad, the highest point in San Diego, overlooks the ocean and La Jolla, a small community just north of downtown. It was there in July 1962, just below the huge cross that towers over the city, that I stopped to thank God as I headed to the church for my wedding ceremony. Joan and I have returned to Mount Soledad many times over the years to thank our loving God for the many blessings He has given us.

I hope you have some special place in your life where you can find solitude in His presence. It is a perfect way to thank God — or seek His guidance. It is also how you discover that God draws close to you in these moments of major decision. You literally can feel His presence.

It has been more than forty-five years since that fateful trip west, yet I recall clearly that electric moment when I drove over the foothills east of San Diego and caught my first glimpse of the Pacific Ocean twenty-five miles ahead. There is something breathless and magical about a clear, sunny day in California.

As I think back, I shudder at the irresponsibility and perhaps arrogance of that bold move. I guess I was either too naïve or just plain reckless, but despite the odds, I just knew that I'd find a job and settle in. To me, this was what faith is all about — trusting God implicitly to meet all our needs. Isn't that the way you *really* want to live? And isn't that what the apostle Paul meant when he said we are to "walk by faith, not by sight" (2 Corinthians 5:7 KJV)? As I think of the generation of twentysomethings who are leaving the church despite being raised in Christian homes, I wonder sometimes if they need to see their parents living more adventurous lives. That's what living by faith is all about.

My first task back then was to find a place to live. Having driven 2,500 miles to be near the ocean, I was determined to live as close to it as possible. As luck would have it, I found a sweet elderly landlady who allowed me to move into a small efficiency apartment a half block from the Windansea beach in La Jolla. As it turned out, she had been a passionate Nixon supporter and wanted to help the cause even in defeat, so she gave me three months to pay the rent.

Soon I found temporary work with a firm specializing in government relations, and several months later, with the encouragement of newspaper owner Jim Copley, I joined Copley Newspapers, where my first job was to maintain retirement records for its some 5,000 employees. Thus my newspaper career was launched.

Now, the way I described it, you might say I fell into my newspaper career by accident, and it does sort of seem that way. But I have to believe that my willingness to obey that voice inside my heart, which I regard as God at work in me, led me on an amazing adventure that continues to this day. And I truly believe that Christians can experience that same level of adventure today if they follow their hearts, for God usually speaks to the heart rather than the head.

ON THE RECORD

Choking Off Life

To the degree that we allow ourselves to suffer anxiety, fear, self-condemnation, and self-hate, we literally choke off the life force available to us and we turn our back upon the gift which our Creator has made.

Dr. Maxwell Maltz
Author of *Psycho-Cybernetics*

As I think about this inauspicious arrival on the California scene, I appreciate how fortunate I have been. I had no idea what life would bring, but it never occurred to me that I might fail. Success was not certain, but I was not willing to think about the alternative.

Over the years I have observed many church folk who become paralyzed when faced with important decisions. They tend to either retreat into the status quo or become negative and pessimistic about the future. How sad! Sure, these things can be scary. Quit your job to try something new? Move your family halfway across the country? Take a cut in pay so you can do something that fits your truest self better than what you're doing now? Those are not easy prospects to face, but if God is in it, you will never regret making those changes in your life. No goal is worth its salt if it doesn't involve risk taking and the possibility of failure, yet you can't get there without an optimistic spirit. You don't have a prayer if you think you are destined to fail before you even start.

Too many Christians waste too much energy complaining about things they cannot change and hoping for something they cannot have. Such unhappy people miss so much of life in the process. But worse, they become billboards for our faith advertising what no one wants.

When you tap your optimistic potential, you are able to take an important personal decision and lift it to even higher levels of achievement. Think back on your first day in a new job. Were you scared? Did you worry that you had made a mistake? Did you think your new boss gave you credit for talent and experience you did not possess? Did you have doubts about whether you could turn in the first-class performance you were expected to deliver? Of course you did, and that's when an optimistic approach can make all the difference in the world.

In retrospect, I was, in varying degrees, unqualified for most of the jobs I took on in my career, but I just sensed that I was right where God wanted me to be and that He would help me grow into each new opportunity. And you know what? He did! Trusting God: that's what faithful living is all about.

As a green and unproven junior officer, I reported aboard my first ship — a destroyer operating off Okinawa — and was put in charge of a division of forty men. I was twenty-two years old and had never managed anyone other than myself. In 1961 I joined Copley Newspapers with absolutely no training in journalism, but it soon became my career. Eight years later I took on a major responsibility for the government and found myself way in over my head as a "retired" Navy lieutenant junior grade moving into the office of the secretary of defense with a Marine general as my assistant. I was scared to death, but by golly, I was going to succeed. I had no choice but to prove I could make the grade.

In 1979 Knight Ridder asked me to become senior vice president of newspaper operations. The corporate headquarters were located in the state-of-the-art facilities of its flagship newspaper, *The Miami*

Herald. I had been meticulously screened, interviewed for hours, and cross-examined by an army of Knight Ridder executives and became the pick of the litter. Once again, I was stretching into a major responsibility well beyond my professional experience. But I optimistically moved ahead. Throughout the decision process, I felt the hand of God leading me along.

For years I had admired Knight Ridder as the best in the business. It was a first-class organization, universally respected for high ethical standards and commitment to excellence. I was moving into a job six times larger in scope than my prior work, and I would travel the country, overseeing some of the nation's best and largest newspapers. Sure, I had an enormous amount to learn, but I felt I could grow into the job. Again, I would give another new challenge my best shot. The message was clear: Think positive, believe in yourself, and go for it. I was determined to grab that brass ring. And I thanked God for yet another wonderful opportunity in life.

My thirteen-year newspaper career in South Florida included seven years as publisher of *The Miami Herald,* during which we won five Pulitzer prizes and were selected twice as one of the top ten newspapers in the country. But the job turned out to be one of the most rigorous in the country, one for which no one could be fully prepared. That is often the case in life — all the more reason to be optimistic and remain optimistic, especially when under fire.

By 1991 I had been in the newspaper industry for thirty years and our younger daughter was off to college. So, for the first time in years, my wife and I could move without pulling anyone out of

ON THE RECORD

Optimism Can Be a Lifesaver

In public service you must be an optimist, because if you weren't the job would kill you.

Merrett Stierheim
Former manager of Miami Dade County

school. We were empty nesters, ready to reestablish our western roots. It was a perfect time to repot. My goal was to pursue a new and different life — writing books, serving on corporate boards, and reuniting my family. All this took a huge leap of faith and a substantial dose of optimism, but we realized that there was so much more life out there and we were ready to accept new challenges. Yet, unbeknownst to us, God had other plans. Just as we were packing up for our trip west, another unexpected surprise came our way: a call from President George H. W. Bush to become his ambassador to Spain.

The announcement that I was leaving Miami caught the attention of the president. We had been friends since his days as a congressman, when I served in the Pentagon, and we had stayed in close touch ever since. Joan and I admired the dedication and integrity of Barbara and George Bush and strongly supported the Bush administration's foreign policy.

Spain seemed a perfect fit for us. We had strong roots there: Joan had been an exchange student in Barcelona during high school, and we both were conversational in Spanish. Best of all, 1992 was an incredibly important year for Spain, involving the Summer Olympic Games in Barcelona, a world's expo in Seville, and a yearlong celebration of the discovery of America by Christopher Columbus. I would need all the energy and uplifting spirit I could muster. We were there to represent our country, and it was a great honor for this kid from Queens, New York. Once again the hand of God was at work in our lives.

But then again, all great adventures in life eventually end. Ours did, rather abruptly: when George H. W. Bush lost his bid for reelection, I lost my job. So in February 1993, Joan and I returned to Southern California. She enrolled in a master's program at Westminster Theological Seminary, and I agreed to serve on several corporate boards and also to write a book (*Finish Strong*, published in 1996).

I hesitate to put all this down on paper, but my point is this: I was a nobody from a humble background, yet somewhere along the way I sensed God's claim on my life. There is absolutely no way I could have planned the exciting career I have had. Instead, I had a simple trust in God and followed His leading even when it didn't make sense. I realize that my own experiences might seem extraordinary, and I surely do not want to come off as a "name it and claim it" kind of guy. But I think I can guarantee on the basis of Scripture that if you put your complete trust in God for everything — your spouse, your job, your dreams — you will experience things beyond your wildest imagination. And in the process you will demonstrate to others an appealing abandonment of convention that strikes at the core of our faith.

ON THE RECORD

How to Avoid Moral Bankruptcy

If the firm does not have a moral reference point, it has the potential to contribute to the bankruptcy of the human soul. We have been created in God's image, and the results of our leadership will be measured beyond the workplace. The story will be told in the changed lives of people.

Bill Pollard
Former chairman and CEO, ServiceMaster

The neat thing is that God continues to lead us into new adventures. I am very proud of Joan's courage in heading back to graduate school more than thirty years after completing her undergraduate work in college. With the inspiration of a wonderful Bible teacher in Miami, she had developed her own talents as a dedicated teacher of the Old and New Testaments, and armed with a master's degree in theology, she felt she would be better prepared for her work. With considerable trepidation she returned to the campus, facing professors who were mostly younger than she and students who were younger than our children. Of no surprise to me, she quickly earned everyone's respect and took on her studies with commitment and passion, even the required years of Hebrew and ancient Greek.

In each chapter of our lives together, Joan and I have been reminded time and again that behind it all is a loving God opening opportunity's door and guiding us along the way. It was the Lord who gave us courage and reassurance. It was He who helped us overcome doubts and fears as we took on new challenges that seemed far beyond our experience or skills. Knowing that He is on our side, that He is directing our actions, that His love is unconditional provides unbelievable peace even in turbulent times. There is a quiet sense of comfort just knowing that He directs our every move. It is likely that we will live in an uncertain world of turbulence and violence for the rest of our days. And that's why it's important to keep our focus on His grace. James 1:12 says,

> Blessed is the man who perseveres under trial, because when he has stood the test, he will receive the crown of life that God has promised to those who love him.

Often tough decisions are lonely moments. Your friends and family may have differing views, and that makes your decision even tougher. One of the hardest things I have learned in life is that you cannot please everyone all the time. Growing up in a dysfunctional family environment, I had an enormous need to be appreciated and praised. I wanted to be liked, to be popular with everyone. I wanted everyone to agree with me, even though that was impossible. First and foremost, I found that you must be yourself. You must know who you are and what you believe — and be willing to stand up for those principles that you believe define who you are. And you must trust in God.

Life's journey as a Christian can be lonely and difficult. Too often we allow personal distractions and other worldly priorities to dominate. We rely too much on our own energies and personal resources to get by. When life is good, we may fail to credit our Savior for our many blessings, and when problems arise, we worry plenty but fail to turn our concerns over to God.

So let me be very honest. Like many Christians, I went through a period when I paid more attention to my agenda than to God's. I trusted too much in myself and not enough in Him. For the first few years of our marriage, Joan and I described ourselves as Christians, but we seldom stopped to acknowledge how little we really knew about our faith. Sure, we had been baptized, confirmed, and married in the presence of God, family, and friends. We went to church and prayed regularly, but something was missing.

All that changed when we moved to Miami and met Dan Yeary, senior pastor of University Baptist Church. Dan was an inspiring preacher who demanded intensive study of the Bible. His sermons were Christ-focused and challenging. No "cultural Christians" could escape his message. The Bible was his central road map, and he taught its message week in and week out. Thanks to Dan, we grew enormously in understanding the Word and returned our focus to Jesus Christ.

Dan rebaptized each member of our family in rededication of our lives to our loving God. We were born again. Later, on our twenty-fifth wedding anniversary — in the presence of our pastor, our children, and the Lord — we renewed our marriage vows in a private ceremony in our church. There we recommitted our lives to each other, to our children, and to our Lord, who had blessed us so abundantly.

I mention this because I know you also will face times of spiritual dryness. Even now, you may feel distant from God. When that happens, we should never despair, nor should we ignore the emptiness we feel. That is God's way of trying to get our attention. In my case, it involved a new church and a pastor bold enough to confront us with our need to take our faith to the next level. But what it really took was for me to swallow my pride and admit that I had let my faith go soft.

If you sense that you have fallen away from a vibrant relationship with God, don't let pride get in the way of returning to His side.

Bill Hoeveler, one of America's most respected federal judges, suffered a severe stroke five years ago. He said, "I have been dished out this severe stroke and I must deal with it. I find people respond much more favorably, and thus give me hope, when they see me as optimistic." Soon afterward, his wife of more than forty years died after a brief illness. Bill's world was turned upside down, but there was no giving up. Through it all, Judge Hoeveler, who faithfully attended with me a men's Bible study group that met in Miami every other Friday, has shown enormous courage and faith: "The older I become and the more I read and pray, the more I understand that there can be no real love nor honesty without a real faith in God."

I believe that God has an adventure for every one of His followers. It is right there for the taking for those who will put their complete trust in Him. It will not necessarily be a life of material wealth or worldly success. But if you follow His leading and obey that still, small voice in your heart, you too will be able to say with me, "Wow! What a ride this is!"

ON THE RECORD

How to Smile Again

Everyone has moments of pain, weakness, and insecurity. Remember they don't last forever. Sometimes it takes the darker moments for us to realize later how wonderful our life actually is. Keep a positive attitude, and before you know it, you will have things to smile about again.

Caroline Parler
Columbia, South Carolina

When you trust in God, you see the world with new eyes because you know He leads the way.

FAITH KEEPERS

How to Build Trust

- Start the day by thanking God for all your many blessings.
- Give someone a happy day, and you will receive one in return.
- Don't focus on what you don't have. Doing so will frustrate you and make you appear ungrateful.
- Look at the sunny side of everything. Attitude determines how much of the future you will be allowed to see and to enjoy.
- Be a friend and lean on one too.
- Forgive an injustice.
- Listen more and be kind.
- Remember that happiness is largely under your control. There is little correlation between the circumstances of your life and how happy you can be.
- Face up to problems and resolve them.
- Focus on small moments so that you can better appreciate what's really important.
- Nurture your faith in a loving God — every day.

Chapter 2

TREAT YOURSELF TO A FAITH LIFT

UNBLEMISHED LEGACY

In a world where change seems the only constant, the most precious gold of all is to be found in those unchanging values that ultimately dwarf the outward signs of material success....

Material possessions rust away, wear away, or depreciate. Character alone will never tarnish.

Charles Colson, founder of Prison Fellowship Ministries

GOD'S INFINITE MAKEOVER

Either you look at the universe as a very poor creation out of which no one can make anything, or you look at your own life and your own part in the universe as infinitely rich, full of inexhaustible interest, opening out into infinite further possibilities.... Beyond all and in all is God.

Thomas Merton, teacher, author, and Trappist monk

MIRED DOWN IN THE MATERIAL

Without God we are mired in the material.... Without God there is a coarsening of the society. Without God democracy will not and cannot endure. If we forget that we are one nation under God, then we will be a nation gone under.

President Ronald Reagan, at the 1984 National Prayer Breakfast

Reality television shows seem to be the rage these days. Each week millions are glued to the tube watching these programs that promise money, fame, and instant success to the winners. One is left with the sense that the good life comes easily — at least for some.

For most of us, that's not true at all, because God requires commitment and a faith that goes deep. As far as He is concerned, there are no shortcuts in the service of the Lord. "To whom much is given, much is expected," the Bible says (see Luke 12:48).

Nevertheless, many of us seek the easy way out — instant fame, a quick buck, overnight success. More than 40 million Americans watch and vote on *American Idol* some weeks. Another big hit, *Extreme Makeover*, features teams of home repair people who sweep in and almost overnight remodel rundown homes of needy people. *The Apprentice* promotes ruthless competition and the humiliating "You're fired!" from Donald Trump, who personifies glitz and excess. And then there's *Survivor*, promoting the concept that the way to satisfaction (and a million dollars) is found by misleading, cheating, and reneging on commitments to others.

ON THE RECORD

A Heart Faith Lift

It is not what I do that matters but what a sovereign God chooses to do through me. God doesn't want worldly success. He wants my heart, in submission to Him. Life is not just a few years to spend on self-indulgence and career advancement.

It's a privilege, a responsibility, a stewardship to be lived according to a much higher calling — God's calling. This alone gives true meaning to life.

U.S. Senator Elizabeth Dole, North Carolina

When I first heard about the network feature *The Swan*, it seemed unbelievable. This show sought out the most physically unattractive person it could find and then, in front of millions of viewers, transformed that individual into a beautiful woman through the miracle of reconstructive surgery, professional grooming, and a brand-new wardrobe. Before millions of curious viewers the show figuratively turned an ugly duckling into a swan.

It bothers me that so many people truly believe that the good life comes in such cruel and superficial ways. Is this the answer to filling our life with meaning? Is this what God promises those who have placed their lives in His hands?

How could anyone put themselves through such surgical and psychological torture or be totally humiliated by *American Idol* judges or the arbitrary judgments of a Donald Trump? And worse yet, are we as viewers so jaded that it takes a show like this to get us to tune in? It's almost like the old amusement park "freak shows" where people paid a quarter to catch a glimpse of some poor soul who had a horrible physical deformity. In essence, that's what these "makeover" shows do.

I think the success of these shows says something profound about us: we love simple answers and dramatic turnarounds, whether it's from poor to rich, homely to beautiful, sad to happy, or tragic to triumphant. We seem to gain inspiration from watching the transformation of bad to good, and we especially like it when the recipient has done nothing to earn it. It just comes out of the blue.

Too often we come to think that our needs are met with more money, more fame, a higher-paying job, or more power. Yet the more we get, the more dissatisfied we become — and life remains an empty shell. When that happens, we desperately need a faith lift, a complete makeover of the soul.

God never promised us an easy life on the beach in the sun. Rather, He requires that we grow and renew our faith every

ON THE RECORD

Discover Your Purpose

The One who caused you to be created, created you for a cause. Get to know Him personally and find out what He wants you to do.

Ty Miller
Property manager,
Rancho Santa Fe, California

day and that we radiate His love wherever we might be — at work, at church, in our neighborhoods, at school, with friends. He expects us to reach for the stars and to test our energies and talents. He wants us to use our time on earth wisely and reminds us repeatedly that there are no free tickets in our journey of faith.

This means hard work. If we are not in shape for the task, then we need a crash spiritual fitness program to make it, especially when we must deal with tough times.

When I was a kid, I didn't have much. I grew up in Queens, New York. The streets were crowded and tough, as thousands of European immigrants flooded to the cheap tenements of our neighborhood. With my parents divorced, my mom raised my little brother and me all by herself. Every day she rode the subway for two hours to get to work and back, often not getting home until ten or eleven at night so she could get some overtime pay.

To supplement the family income, I washed windows for two bucks an apartment. One summer I made $500, which translated into 1,750 windows. I remember that precise number fifty years later as if it were a terrible nightmare, and I've hated washing windows ever since. But that might have been the highlight of my young career, as it seemed to go downhill from there. My next job was on a housewrecking crew. And after that, I got a job driving a garbage truck.

I was just like every other kid on my block. Poor. Not particularly talented. And going absolutely nowhere. It was only two years after World War II, and most Americans were struggling to get back on

ON THE RECORD

Personal Example

Having become a Christian helped me as a leader understand grace, peace, and assurance. It is not what we say in company memos or at the podium that defines our values and assures those around us. It's what we do, day in and day out. And we earn that respect when things are tough, not when they are going well.

Jim Carreker
Former CEO, Wyndham Hotels, Dallas, Texas

their feet. In school I was an average student. In fact, I had little confidence that I could ever do well in school. To tell the truth, I was pretty much convinced that I couldn't succeed at anything.

And then came just the lift I needed: Wally Manheimer.

Wally was a talented math teacher in our otherwise ordinary school. For whatever reason, he singled me out and started to turn me around. Unlike the reality shows, he didn't use a scalpel or makeup artist. Nor did he promise me an easy answer or a free ticket to the honor roll. Instead, he went to work on my intellect — which would involve hard work. Somehow he saw something inside me that I didn't know was there, and he tapped into it by getting me to start taking my education seriously. Wally convinced me I could amount to something.

ON THE RECORD

Above All Else

I consider faith to be primarily a gift from God, nurtured and fostered by my family. For me it provides a framework and constancy. All of life's decisions, activities, structure can be made in light of my underlying faith.

Dr. Joe Bliss
Research physician specializing in infectious diseases, and *USA Today* honoree

With Wally pushing me, I began to get better grades. In fact, by my junior year, I had improved so much that I made the honor roll. Through his confidence in me, this special teacher had empowered me to succeed. For the first time in my life, I began to dream about college. There was no way my mother could afford to send me; this was before there were special grants and loan packages to help poor kids like me go to college. Still, I persevered because Wally told me to believe in myself and said that if I earned really good grades I might get a scholarship.

Sure enough, I applied to the Navy for an NROTC scholarship, and on April 3, 1953, a letter from the U.S. Navy arrived with the unbelievable news: I had just won a full ride — tuition, room and board, and living expenses for four years!

Fast-forward to my office here in California. There is a picture on the wall of me standing next to President George H. W. Bush on the occasion of his appointing me as his ambassador to Spain. As I look at that picture and reflect on the privilege I had in representing our country abroad and, earlier, as publisher of a major daily newspaper, I have to pinch myself. How did that poor kid in a tenement in Queens end up here?

It's that ever-popular story again. The ugly duckling turns into a swan. Not necessarily because the duckling deserved it, but because of a gift. A random tap on the shoulder and a voice that says, "You're not going to believe what I have for you." God tells us that too.

I'm not sure why Wally Manheimer reached out to me, but I think it had more to do with him than with me. That is, I don't think I had any more potential than any of the other guys or girls in that class. He just loved seeing a spark ignite in his students and offered a chance to whoever would take it. He saw his life's purpose as being an enabler, a helper. Most of us can remember special teachers who influenced us for good the way Wally Manheimer did.

The Lord has an amazing knack for bringing good people into your life — uplifters who seem to arrive on the scene just when you need help the most. As I look back on that math teacher's concern for me, I am absolutely convinced it was the hand of a loving God at work.

Have you ever had that same thought as you reflect on some special experience that changed your life? Do you really think it was an accident or

ON THE RECORD

Depending on You

Pray for wisdom in knowing which dreams to pursue. Then pray for opportunities to meet people who can help the dreams become reality. In the meantime, study and work as though everything depends upon you.

**Michael Lindsey
Gallup Poll consultant
and Princeton Theological
Seminary graduate**

coincidence? Or was it the grace of God's embrace, protecting and guiding your actions?

So how can you become God's very presence in the lives of others? The word *presence* implies that you "are there" for others. Available. How many times have you been in too much of a hurry when someone began to share something personal with you? One thing you may need to do is slow down and be willing to enter into the lives of people beyond the superficial relationships you have at work and in your neighborhood.

It is important just to be there and to listen. Only then can you find the opening to share from your heart a message of comfort or hope. Often it is in a time of crisis that someone you never thought you had much of a relationship with reaches out to you. Someone at work breaks down because her husband is dying. A neighbor's teenage son is on drugs and comes to you for advice. It is not a coincidence that they reached out to you. God has given you an opportunity to be His arms and legs here on earth. There can be no procrastination, no avoidance. The crisis is *now*, and you are the person to deal with it. Remember that God is working through you. This is a gift for you to share, especially in moments of trauma and suffering. As Paul wrote to the believers in Galatia, we are to "carry each other's burdens" (Galatians 6:2).

The Lord asks us to serve Him, and He isn't likely to make it easy or comfortable. There simply are too many needs in this world, and He may want us to be in the darkest places of the secu-

ON THE RECORD

Eternal Love

If we work upon marble, it will perish; if we work upon brass, time will efface it; if we rear temples, they will crumble to dust; but if we work upon immortal minds, if we imbue them with principles, with just fear of God and love of our fellow men, we engrave on those tablets something which will brighten to all eternity.

Daniel Webster
Congressman, U.S. senator, secretary of state

lar world, where we can radiate the light of His love. This can be hard work, and lonely too. Sometimes you may never see results in your work, but the Lord expects you to persevere. Maybe you have prayed for twenty years for a friend to find God, but the barrier has been too great. Just remember, it is your task to show others His promise — the Lord will do the rest. The best we can offer to those who are not in the Spirit is love, prayer, and friendship without conditions.

You can partner in God's work by going out into the world in His name. In essence He says, "I want you to touch someone else with My love, and I will empower you for that task."

Somebody . . .

> — Is thinking of you.
> — Cares about you.
> — Misses you.
> — Wants to talk to you.
> — Wants to be with you.
> — Hopes you aren't in trouble.
> — Is thankful for the support you have provided.
> — Wants to hold your hand.
> — Hopes everything turns out all right.
> — Wants you to be happy.
> — Wants you to find him/her.
> — Is celebrating your successes.
> — Wants to give you a gift.
> — Thinks that you ARE a gift.
> — Loves you.
> — Admires your strength.
> — Is thinking of you and smiling.
> — Wants to be your shoulder to cry on.

God reminds us that He is the author of hope and encouragement. He will open doors to amazing opportunity. If you need guidance, He will send you a mentor. And upon their receiving His gift, the transformation begins. No strings attached. Just accept the gift. It's God's way of empowering you for life.

I can say this, not as a theologian — I am not one, nor do I pretend to be — but as someone who has learned (sometimes the hard way) of the power of an unshakable faith in a God who helps me look at each day with hope and gratitude.

So let's look at this gift of faith. My assumption is that you already know a lot about it. Maybe you went to Sunday school as a youngster, or you tried church for a while. Or maybe you regularly attend church but for some reason feel as if you're just going through the motions. Deep inside, you yearn for something more.

My goal is not to turn you into an evangelist or make you quit your job to become a missionary. My goal is to help you connect your faith with everyday life so that you have a sense of purpose and well-being. A spiritual makeover, if you will.

Perhaps you too need a Wally Manheimer to come along and light up your life. Maybe you are the one who hungers for that spiritual makeover, one that is deep with meaning and purpose. Or perhaps your life is in a rut and you are drifting into complacency or depression. Life can be like that — tough or boring. And your walk with God just doesn't do it. Clearly, it's time for renewal — and a faith lift too.

ON THE RECORD

Discovering a Larger Purpose

Through a growing faith we discover a larger perspective, a purpose for our life. We have more energy. Our talents and experience can be used in more powerful ways. Living life without the power of God is like trying to drive on the freeway in neutral with the engine revving.

Rev. Steve Murray
Pastor, La Jolla Community Church, California

In the mix of these conflicting winds of trauma and change, there remains a desperate need to get our lives in order. That was exactly what happened to David Kennedy, whose older brother was killed in the Vietnam War. For Dave, then sixteen, it was a devastating blow. "Out of this whole experience," David told me, "I came to value the nobility of unrecognized effort. You don't perform for the applause. You perform because it is the right thing to do."

That's what God expects from us: Just do the right thing. David Kennedy, a strong family man who had a career as a Navy test pilot, now serves as a consultant to Hollywood producers on films that feature the military. His character has been deeply influenced by his brother's example. Here's how he puts it:

> Integrity is a requisite in determining the fiber and character of an individual and an organization. Integrity demands that there be no twilight zone — something is either right or it is wrong, it is black or it is white.... Integrity requires scourging moral courage, magnetized by fervor for an ideal. To reflect integrity is to invite trust. To possess integrity is to command respect. Morals. Ethics. Standards. Integrity. From these flow a torrent of values. Deeds, not words. Integrity isn't a sometimes thing. It is everything.

In his recent bestseller *All for Jesus*, evangelist Franklin Graham links that integrity to God's work: "There is nothing like the power of integrity. It is a characteristic so radiant, so steady, so consistent, so beautiful that it makes a permanent picture in our mind."

ON THE RECORD

Leading a Balanced Life

My goal is to lead a balanced life: faithful in those habits of prayer, work, study, physical exercise, eating, and sleep which I believe the Holy Spirit has shown me to be right.... Make the wonderful contribution to the world for which you were made, and to which you were meant to give.

Larry Dye
Attorney, Washington, DC

Character is molded out of a lifetime of good deeds. Each deed involves a decision, one that will cause us to move closer to God.

If you look at the lives of some of the great biblical heroes, you will see that it was not unusual for them to have periods when they felt distant from God and experienced dry spells in their faith. That's actually very comforting to me, because there have been times when I just didn't feel all that spiritual.

So consider this one of those times when you take stock of your relationship with God and make the kinds of adjustments that put you back where you belong. The apostle Paul says it well: "For we are God's workmanship, created in Christ Jesus to do good works, which God prepared in advance for us to do" (Ephesians 2:10).

That's what I hope this book will do for you — lead you to "good works." Then you will be reconnected with your faith in God, and He will thus empower you for great purposes.

FAITH KEEPERS

With a Faith Lift ...

- We draw closer to God — and to each other.
- We know there is a purpose to our life — and are comforted by the thought.
- We ask ourselves the hard questions — and adjust our path in life.
- We confess our needs and hurts — and move on.
- We restore ourselves — and become more assured.
- We acknowledge our dependence on God — and receive the gift of eternal life.

Making Over Our Priorities

- Be Principled — Without having the courage of your convictions, you can't have credibility or character.

- Be Trustworthy — Don't cheat, steal, deceive, or lie.

- Keep Promises — Fulfill commitments; don't try to sneak out of pledges using phony loopholes.

- Be Loyal — To friends, family, colleagues at work, the boss, clients, and country.

- Be Fair — Show your commitment to justice, equal treatment, and acceptance of diversity.

- Care for Others — Be kind and compassionate in helping those in need.

- Respect Others — Be courteous and decent; never embarrass or demean.

- Pursue Excellence — Be your best, diligent, industrious, reliable, and well-informed. No halfhearted performances allowed.

- Radiate Your Faith — Don't forget that everyone around you is watching.

Chapter 3

EMBRACE CHANGE

CHANGE IS NEVER EASY

This has not been an easy transition to make, but with the help of one's family and one's friends, and with the conviction that God works his own purposes in each of our lives, it is easier to see that leaving the White House is not the end of the world but simply the beginning of a new chapter in one's life.

**President Gerald R. Ford, several months
after being defeated in the election of 1976**

GOD'S WORK

With good conscience our only sure reward, with history the final judge of our deeds, let us go forth ... knowing that here on earth God's work must truly be our own.

**President John F. Kennedy,
inaugural address, January 1961**

DEEDS — GREAT AND SMALL

God gives all some work to do — if not great deeds, then small ones — as the cup of cold water to one of His children. Yes, even less than that — a word of advice, something lent to another, a little vexation patiently borne, the fault or thoughtlessness of another repaired without his knowledge. God will recompense it all a thousandfold.

**Jane Stanford, words carved into the walls
of the Stanford University Chapel built in memory
of her son "to the glory of God"**

When Joan picked up the phone in late November 1968, the caller claimed to be Congressman Mel Laird. My wife thought it was a joke. The morning front pages across America had shown Mel, a close friend, standing alongside President-elect Richard Nixon, who had just announced his selection for secretary of defense. Certainly the new secretary of defense was not calling us! We were wrong. One of Mel's first moves was to select a handful of key aides to help in the task, and he wanted me to join his team.

I protested by citing my lack of experience, my roots in California, and the ages of my young family, but Mel would hear none of my excuses. "Dick, I need you for this assignment. I want people around me I can trust implicitly. Get on the next flight to Washington and we'll discuss it."

Sometimes the great opportunities of life come along when you least expect them or want them. I am reminded of God's command to Moses to go into the Promised Land, but Moses, who felt unprepared, asked that another be sent. If you want to be where God can use you for His purpose, you need to be alert to those opportunities, and you need to embrace the changes that come with those opportunities. Sometimes God sends you on some very unfamiliar assignments into very tough places.

Every one of my objections to Secretary Laird was valid, and had I not followed his "order" to drop everything and go to Washington, I might still be selling newspapers in California. Not that there's anything wrong with that. But I wonder how many of us are willing to sit back, take

ON THE RECORD

The Lord's Empowerment

When you rely on the Lord and His sovereign purposes and don't care who gets the credit for actions taken, the Lord blesses and empowers in a mighty way.

Bob Singleton
Miami, Florida

the easy way, and ignore what God expects from us. Mel Laird was about to empower me for a huge growth experience.

How about you? Are you afraid of change? Will you take a chance? Do you avoid new adventures because where you are now is safe, even if it is not enabling your best potential? Are you open to that still, small voice of God, who may be telling you it's time to try something new?

Over the years I have learned two things about change. First, it is inevitable. The entire planet is changing, and along with it, your job, your family, the economy, the workplace, and technology. You can't avoid change, because it is happening all around you. Second, we all have a choice about our role in change. We can choose to embrace it, engage it, and welcome it into our lives. Or we can try to escape it, resist it, and fight it.

When Saul's soldiers faced the Philistine giant, Goliath, they were confronted with a major change in their lives. Their comfortable world came to an abrupt halt, and they had to make a decision. Like many of us, they tried the age-old tactic of indecision. "He's too big and powerful. We can never defeat him. We might as well just get used to becoming slaves to the Philistines." But David, a shepherd, took another approach. He accepted the reality of their situation and decided he would rather die fighting than accept being dominated by the Philistines.

Going to Washington and joining the Defense Department was my Goliath. There were plenty of risks, and it seemed that my best option was to back away. Stay put. Take the safer route. Looking back, I'm glad that Secretary Laird talked me into accepting a new challenge, because I learned a power-

ON THE RECORD

God's Dreams for You

Make sure that your dreams are God's dreams for your life. When your dreams are the same as the Father's, He will equip you and guide you to their fulfillment.

Tal Prince
USA Today honoree,
Birmingham, Alabama

ful lesson from that experience: God does not lead you into new challenges and then leave you hanging. I almost declined the offer, because it seemed too daunting a challenge. Yet it scares me now to think what might have happened if I had given in to my fears.

Despite the enormity of my duties as a public servant in the Pentagon, I was able to live out my faith in an environment I had never dreamed was possible. My unexpected appointment to the Defense Department predictably turned out to be a major turning point in my career. New opportunities opened up, and with them my perspective on life grew enormously. I learned a great deal from some amazing leaders, starting with Mel Laird, who has been a key mentor in my life. My wife and I grew even closer as we prayed together during those difficult times of transition for our family.

What about you? What is your first response when something new comes your way? Are you an "early adapter," or are you the type to wait and see how everyone else does before you jump? During my experience in business and politics I seldom saw Christians as being the ones eager to embrace change. They had the reputation of being satisfied with the way things were. Yet, imagine the power we could unleash if every person who goes to church on Sunday began looking for new ways to live out their faith. To get out of their comfort zone. To soar majestically, just like eagles.

It might be something as simple as determining to do something nice for two or three of your neighbors. Or to raise your hand when your small-group leader asks for volunteers to lead the group in her absence. Or to yield to an inner desire and join in with a group in your church that is planning a mission trip to Central America. But at the same time you have a 101 reasons why you should just maintain your routine.

What if those opportunities were part of God's plan for you to "shine like stars" (Philippians 2:15)? If you could bring just one person into a deeper relationship with God, would you do it? Are you willing to show in everyday ways that followers of Jesus are not the dull, boring, judgmental people we are often caricatured as? Jesus never played it safe, which is why He attracted so many followers. Wouldn't it be great if the people in your circle of influence — neighbors, co-workers, friends outside of church — knew you as someone who loved life and experienced it to the fullest? That will never happen if you make safety and security your ultimate goals.

In his inspiring book *Halftime*, Bob Buford encourages people approaching middle age to begin looking for ways to change their outlook from success to significance. He compares the lives many of us lead to the Israelites under Egyptian bondage: we get up in the morning, go to work making bricks for Pharaoh, go home, eat dinner, go to bed, get up, go to work ... you get the idea. Buford, a friend of strong faith whom I admire greatly, challenges us to plan for some major changes in the second half of life so that we break the cycle of boredom and monotony. What he proposes is indeed scary, but he tells countless stories of people who have done it and discovered a whole new level of fulfillment and enjoyment from life. He also tells several very sad stories of those who were all set to embark on a new way of living but opted for the safety of their current situation.

Too many followers of Jesus are really following the same gods they followed before they encountered Christ: material success, personal power, prestige, and something others call spiritual mediocrity. They try to fit these temporal deities into their Christian faith rather than let their new life in Christ drive them to something better. Our faith is never about mediocrity and settling for something inferior. Intuitively we know this, which is why we are so energized when a visiting missionary tells stories of frontline excitement in the service of Christ. Inwardly, we want the same "high" they get, but that old resistance to change pulls us back into the rut. And then we wonder why the rest of the world doesn't want what we have to offer. We're chasing the same things they are and, just like them, realizing that life isn't about "things."

Former U.S. Senator Bill Armstrong of Colorado learned this lesson on Capitol Hill. As a key Senate leader, he had all the trappings of power flowing from his prestigious public service career, but in due time he found that they were not so important anymore. Much to the surprise of everyone, he announced he was not going to seek reelection. That's not the way things work in politics. In Washington, the Senate is the ultimate club, and once you get in, you do everything you can to stick around for a long time.

Bill had won every office he sought — from the Colorado state legislature to the U.S. House of Representatives and finally two terms in the Senate. He was universally respected and had become a very effective legislator. Willing to persuade and compromise when necessary, he built consensus and got things done.

But Senator Armstrong also took very seriously his relationship with Christ and was a dedicated leader in Bible study groups on Capitol Hill and in the National Prayer Breakfast. He shared his faith publicly and contagiously, but he hungered for more time to spend on areas of life that he felt had more significance than political office — time to be with his family, to study God's Word and grow in his faith, and to be able to serve God more effectively as a private citizen. That takes guts. It's one thing to leave the Senate to

ON THE RECORD

God's Hometown

God instructs us to value our communities. One of the reasons we exist is to relate to other human beings.... My first priority is honoring God, doing everything that is good and pleasing to Him.

Diamond Arnold
Research associate, Ken Blanchard Companies, Escondido, California

take a cabinet position or run for president. But to serve God and be with his family?

I spoke with Bill during this transition, and what was particularly admirable to me was his calm, humble focus. He knew his priorities, and he knew his Lord. He was totally at peace. His anchor lay not in the transitory nature of Washington politics but rather in things eternal. He had no trouble leaving behind the temporary trappings of public life, because he knew who he was in the eyes of his Lord and Savior. As is often the case when any of us are in a time of change, this was a lonely decision, but Bill was determined to bring the priorities of his life into balance.

ON THE RECORD

Crossroads

At each crossroads I come to, I try to do two things: Ask for God's guidance and remember how others will be affected by my decision.

**Anne-Marie Oreskovich
Spokane, Washington**

In an era when fame and fortune seem to rule, it's refreshing to know people like Bill Armstrong who serve and move on. His example of feet-on-the-ground humility provided great encouragement to me as I worked to find balance in my own life.

Most of us can embark on new adventures only in small increments, and that's okay. In fact, that's life in the real world. You are given an additional responsibility at work. You decide to improve your knowledge of the Internet and use it to expand your mind. You try a new sport or travel to a little-known part of the world. You volunteer at church or work for a community-based cause. You seek opportunities to learn and grow. You develop a mind-set that faces every change in your life with enthusiasm rather than dread.

When was the last time you jumped up and tried to touch the "ceiling" of your life? If it has been more than a year since you tried something new, it's time to actively look for a new challenge. You will be surprised at how doing something out of the ordinary can begin a process that will literally recharge your life. At the same time, the longer you stay where you are, the harder it will be to leave that safe yet uninspired lifestyle. Once you take the plunge, you will discover energy you never thought you had. Things around you come alive, and your spirits soar. People are more interesting, and the job more fun.

Positive change also comes from serving others. Help a kid in trouble. Deliver meals to shut-ins. Serve soup to the homeless. Work for a candidate for public office. Read the Bible with a friend. Go to church or join a small prayer group. Pray for someone who's dying. Share special memories. Reunite with long-lost friends. Call someone you love. Create new traditions within your family.

If your life is full of problems and frustrations, identify the biggest ones and develop a practical action plan to solve them. If they can't be solved, accept their inevitability and move on. It's okay to admit that you are not satisfied with your life or job. That's when finding new adventures is so important. Stretch yourself; raise the bar; set new goals.

There are many wonderful things God wants to do in your life. All will require change. Sure, change can be scary — and even unwanted. But I have never met anyone who obeyed God's call to a new challenge and regretted it. As the Bible says,

> Commit to the LORD whatever you do, and your plans will succeed (Proverbs 16:3).

Change is good for the soul. It helps sort out what's truly important in your life — now and in the future. Change forces you to strip away past conveniences and comforts. Maybe you will need to reprove yourself all over again. And that's not all bad! It gets the juices going — new hurdles to climb, new reputations to earn, new friends to make, new legacies to create.

When I was named U.S. Ambassador to Spain, I knew that God was once again at work in my life. The job was a perfect match, given my previous experience, my knowledge of the language, my admiration for the senior President Bush, and my desire to radiate God's love wherever my career path took me. That's why I chose at my State Department swearing-in ceremony on the eve of my arrival in Madrid to read the following passage from the New Testament: "This is the wonderful message he has given us to tell others. We are Christ's ambassadors, and God is using us to speak to you" (2 Corinthians 5:19–20 NLT).

What a fitting reference it was as I stood before leaders of Congress, key presidential advisors, the retired chief justice of the Supreme Court, business leaders, members of the diplomatic corps, and family and friends. Administering my oath was U.S. Circuit Court Judge Peter Fay, my close friend, who for ten years had been in a small men's Bible study group in Miami. Flanking us were the Reverend Billy Graham and the late Richard Halverson, then chaplain of the U.S. Senate, who offered opening and closing prayers for the occasion.

Many friends from the Jewish community were there that day. They knew about my faith and I think respected what I had to say because I had always tried to reflect respect for their beliefs as well. That day God blessed Joan and me with the opportunity to serve — and to witness to His overriding power.

Years ago, while in transition from one job to another, I returned to my old office to pick up something I mistakenly had left behind. It was as if I had never worked there. It took less than twenty-four hours for the building crew to remove the brass nameplate from my office door and paint over my name on that once-coveted executive parking space. Dick Capen was history. That chapter had ended, and the page was turned in short order. Such realities keep you humble and also bring into perspective the things that matter most. As one door closes, others will open. That's the way God works.

That is exactly what Joan and I discovered when we went to Spain. It was an experience we had never anticipated nor sought, but the fit was perfect. We were ready for a new challenge.

We represented our country at dozens of events during the 1992 Summer Olympic Games in Barcelona and entertained more than 7,000 guests at the ambassador's official residence on Castellana, Madrid's Fifth Avenue. We launched a major effort to help American and Spanish businesspeople develop and promote trade between our countries, and we worked hard to extend the interchange of cultural and educational programs.

One of our most ambitious goals was to "show the flag" in all fifty provinces of Spain, where we met with an amazing array of local officials and ordinary citizens who reflected the country's great cultural diversity.

His Majesty King Juan Carlos and President George H. W. Bush had been friends for years, so the rich tradition of presenting my credentials to the king at the Royal Palace was the thrill of a lifetime. There is nothing quite like pulling up to the gates of the palace in His Majesty's eighteenth-century gold-gilded horse-drawn carriage while a Spanish Army Royal Band stands smartly at attention playing our national anthem as I enter. All this for a kid from Queens! It just shows how God leads the way.

We started that day in prayer and arrived at the king's palace with our family Bible in hand. That powerful admonition I had quoted

---

ON THE RECORD

God's Lead

*Do what you feel God leading you to do and trust that His plan is for you to grow and to become the person He made you. The highest calling we have is to mirror God's love through your actions.... I came to see that my faith wasn't necessarily about what God could do **for** me, but what God could do **through** me.*

Carla Barnhill
Editor, *Christian Parenting Today* magazine

during my swearing-in ceremony came alive as never before: "We are Christ's ambassadors, and God is using us to speak to you" (2 Corinthians 5:20 NLT).

Our time in Spain was a very special experience, but I knew the dream would one day end. It is God's way of reminding us of our dependence on Him, not on any slim trappings of power. No more limos or embassy aides to help smooth the way. No Marine Corps honor guard, no driver and bodyguards, no police escorts to get around town. Gone would be my easy access to the centers of power in Madrid and Washington. Yet all those perks are of little importance in the larger picture of life. God had told me it was time to get back to reality.

ON THE RECORD

Enjoy What You Do

In order to be successful, one must find a passion and dedicate his or her energy accordingly. Failure to have fun often results in failure, so don't forget to have fun along the way.

Jerry Richardson
Entrepreneur and owner of the NFL Carolina Panthers

God expects us to use our talents wisely. No one can "coast" his way to heaven. In life we can't always change our circumstances, such as where we work or where we live. It isn't possible for everyone to quit work and move elsewhere. Roots become deep, but the routine doesn't need to become boring or without challenge. God demands that we take advantage of the blessings He has provided — and use them to serve others.

You have the ability to change, to totally transform every area of your life. It all begins as your choice. Procrastinate or act. Do nothing or be decisive. Coast along or make yourself uncomfortable. Carve out new ground or get stuck in your present rut.

I have learned over and over again that God draws close to us in moments of major decisions. He speaks to your heart; you can almost feel His presence, His guiding power. And it brings peace of mind.

What good is it for a man to gain the whole world, yet forfeit his soul? (Mark 8:36).

It is also important to think about how you handle life when the door closes, when life seems to be at a dead end. That's when your true colors emerge. You simply cannot afford to let past failures and disappointments destroy your future.

College administrator Joe White refused to give up when he lost out in the competition to become president of the University of Michigan. He wanted the job more than anything else and felt well prepared for the task. So when he was passed over, the disappointment was huge. Rather than suppress his feelings, he told the world of his sadness and gained universal respect for being so candid. He chose to pick up the pieces and move on. Soon, much to his surprise, an even more exciting opportunity surfaced. Often that's the case. Just when you seem to be staggering along at the bottom of life, a door opens and, with it, a whole new set of wonderful options.

In reflecting on the unwanted and unanticipated change in his life, White, who now heads a major New York investment advisory firm, said, "I am a better leader, more confident, more empathetic, more resilient and wiser for having navigated a major career disappointment."

What a lesson for all of us! Remember that God is at your side reminding you that "there is nothing better for a man than to enjoy his work" (Ecclesiastes 3:22).

It took another form of personal courage when Tim Burke quit professional baseball at the top of his game. A star pitcher for the Montreal Expos, Tim was happily married, but he and his wife could not have children, so they adopted four troubled kids from abroad. All were preschoolers.

His fans were shocked when Tim announced he was leaving the team, but he had it right: "Baseball is going to get along just fine without me, but my children have only one father and my wife only one husband. They need me a lot more than baseball needs me." He was following God's mandate to care for his family.

Casey Lynch was soaring in his high-tech career in Silicon Valley. He had worked hard to earn his MBA at Stanford and was putting in long hours in the office. The promotions came quickly, but each one had its price — mostly at the expense of his family.

One day Casey was offered what he considered the ultimate job, but it meant continued personal sacrifice in order to make large amounts of money. It was a price he was unwilling to pay, so he turned down the job. His friends were shocked: "I basically affirmed a new order of priorities with my family. Health would come before wealth." When people make tough decisions like this, it takes courage — and faith.

When times are tough, when changes need to be made and we feel very much alone, we need to remember that our loving God is our shelter, our protection, our comfort in a storm. With Him always at our side, we are never alone. God gives us the freedom to struggle, to fail, to suffer disappointment and tragedy, but He never leaves us alone. Rather, He gives us courage, strength, encouragement, and hope. We see this in Paul's journey to Rome, when he inspires the crew of his ship not to give up in the face of a huge storm. "So keep up your courage, men, for I have faith in God" (Acts 27:25). Even when we have given up all hope, we must never lose that faith.

Christians ought to be the most change-embracing people on earth. The word that is used to describe what happens when we trust Jesus as our Savior is *transformation*. Change — from old to new, from darkness to light, from purposelessness to purpose. As we grow in our relationship with God and watch for the doors He opens before us, we become adventurers on the most exciting journey on earth.

It is how we travel that journey that attracts others to join us. The way we handle change becomes our "sermon" to those who desperately seek a better way.

What sermon is your life preaching?

FAITH KEEPERS

Turning Your Dreams into God's Purpose for You

- Become a good listener. Great ideas can come from those who inspire you.

- Don't fear change. Welcome it. Encourage it.

- Never stop learning and growing.

- Determine what's important to you.

- Think about what really excites you.

- Manage your free time in ways that bring fulfillment and happiness.

- Face up to mistakes and to things you simply are not capable of doing.

- Don't fear failure. Everything new involves risks — and potential success.

- Develop and maintain a positive attitude. Adversity can defeat you if you let it.

- Stretch your thinking to include all the possibilities open to you.

- Constantly learn and grow, picking up new ideas, new hobbies, and new skills along the way.

- Be sensitive to negative feelings about yourself and drown them out with positive ones.

- Remember, no one can make you feel inferior without your consent.

- Act on your own behalf. Believe in yourself. Encourage yourself.

- Don't procrastinate. When you act, do so with enthusiasm and full energy.

- Be your own best friend.

- Above all, thank God for the blessings of your uniqueness.

Chapter 4

RADIATE GOD'S LOVE

HIS WILL BE DONE

Whatever you do, work at it with all your heart, as working for the Lord, not for men.

Colossians 3:23

WHAT GOD WANTS

My faith demands — this is not optional — that I do whatever I can, wherever I can, whenever I can, for as long as I can, with whatever I have to try to make a difference.

President Jimmy Carter

ULTIMATE FREEDOM

My faith sets me free. Frees me to put my problems of the moment in proper perspective. Frees me to make decisions that others may not like. Frees me to try to do the right thing, even though it might not poll well.

President George W. Bush

GOD'S PLAN

My mother told me that everything in life happened for a purpose. She said it was part of God's plan, even the most disheartening setbacks, and in the end everything works out for the best.

President Ronald Reagan

Remember, my assumption is that you are reading this book because you want something more out of your faith. You want your life to matter, but right now it seems to be stuck on autopilot heading in a direction that is less than satisfying. In chapter 3 we learned that developing an openness to change is the beginning of your journey of empowerment. My guess is that a big change for you will be finding the right ways to become more open with others about your faith. Not in ways that further support the image of Christians as religious zealots only interested in converting others to their point of view, but in genuine acts of love and service to others that spring out of our love for God.

For many years I made the same mistake you may be making. I believed my faith was a personal, private matter that ought to be kept apart from my "real" life in the newsroom. I lived and worked in multiethnic communities represented by many beliefs — as well as by those who claimed no faith at all — and felt I might offend others if I went public with my belief in Jesus. I have since learned that while I should never use my faith as a battering ram to make others believe the way I do, I cannot be an authentic person if I keep my faith in a lockbox. The truth is, it is our obligation to live out our faith in all parts of the world in which we travel.

In the end we simply cannot separate secular life from faith. Yet that is not to say we should thrust our personal views in

ON THE RECORD

Enjoy Each Day

Cherish the precious present. Recognize that happiness and success are not a destiny but a journey. Don't decide you'll be happy when you get the next promotion, or once you get married or buy that house. Instead, relish each day and each moment that you have on earth, because you don't know how long you have.

**Taylor Batten
Newspaper editor,
Charlotte,
North Carolina**

the face of those around us. Quite to the contrary. During the 2000 presidential campaign George W. Bush shocked the media when asked to name the philosopher-thinker he most identified with. Without hesitation he answered, "Jesus Christ, because He changed my heart." In one sentence he had described the inner core of his life, and I feel that he did it in a way that was not offensive or insensitive to others. He was simply being honest.

Whatever your political views, as a Christian you know that we are instructed by Scripture not to be ashamed of the gospel (Romans 1:16). So here's the question: While most people are aware of the president's Christian beliefs, how many of your friends and colleagues outside of church know yours? What might happen if all of us who try to follow Christ let at least one other person know about it and helped them see a "healthy Christian" as opposed to the cartoon-character Christians they see in the media?

We as Christians need to change the stereotype from the dour, judgmental, mean-spirited separatist to the winsome, generous, compelling servant. Many times we are the only "Bible" some people will ever experience, so our personal example is a very important testimony of our faith in God. And it should be so easy.

It is crucial that we live out the principles of the gospel. Loving others. Choosing kindness. Listening before we speak. Perhaps it's a smile or gesture of concern. A pause at someone's desk in the office to ask how things are going. Maybe it's a word of encouragement to someone who is down, or a phone call to a friend in need.

In every community or neighborhood, there are those who just seem to radiate a positive energy. They're the first ones to show up for the blood drive. If a new neighbor moves in, they're at the door with a handshake and a welcome. Neighbor kids like to drop by because they're always greeted with a smile and a listening ear. I'd love to be able to report that these people are always the people who worship in our churches every Sunday, but sadly that isn't always the case.

As Christians we have an obligation to be missionaries in all that we do. And we must be prepared, especially when we least expect the need, to claim the power of our faith. In our small sphere of influence we represent God, sharing with others the blessings He has given us. In so doing, we help others discover God's possibilities for them.

Like everything else worth doing, knowing how to talk about your faith with others will take some careful thought and maybe even a little practice. For example, if someone asked you why you believe the way you do, would you have a ready answer? So the first thing I suggest is that you sit down and write out your "faith story." How did you come to believe the gospel, to accept the truth that Jesus is the Son of God? Was it an instant moment at a revival? Were you led to belief by another person? Was it a gradual process of discovery? And how has it changed your life? How are you different from when you were unable to believe in Christ's love?

ON THE RECORD

The Only Real Power

I really do believe that those of us who are put in positions of public trust really shouldn't be hesitant to speak about spiritual values.... Having a position of power does not bring inner security and fulfillment. That comes only by developing a personal relationship with God.... Inner security and fulfillment come by faith — not by wielding power in the town where power is king.

Former Secretary of State James Baker, at the 1991 National Prayer Breakfast

Write out your story as if you were having a conversation with another person, then practice telling your story to your spouse or a close friend. This may seem a little artificial, but I have found that many Christians avoid talking about their faith to others because they are afraid they won't get it out right. You don't have to be a theologian or a preacher to talk about your faith, but you do need to be prepared. By the simple power of your personal witness, you will bring hope to others.

Judge Peter Fay is one of those very special people who radiates God's love and, in the process, brings hope and optimism to everything he touches. Pete and his wife, Pat, and Joan and I have been close friends for more than twenty-five years and have labored side by side in dealing with some of Miami's most important community issues.

Pete Fay cherishes family values and works hard as a public servant, having served on the federal bench for more than thirty years, twenty of them as a member of the Eleventh Circuit Court of Appeals. In his line of work Judge Fay faces the worst of life — from corruption in business to the ravages of vicious crimes. Yet, no matter what pressures and frustrations his cases bring, Pete projects an uplifting and enthusiastic spirit, anchored in his faith in a loving God.

Even though we now live on opposite coasts, Pete and I remain in close touch by cell phone and frequent reunions. Our conversation is always predictable: "How are you doing, Pete?" I ask. Without fail, his response radiates the optimistic message, "If it gets any better, I wouldn't know what to do."

Always cheerful, always uplifting, Judge Fay stirs a breath of fresh air wherever he goes. At the federal courthouse he is legendary — from prison guards to prosecutors, from law clerks to magistrates. All will tell you about his uplifting powers and caring spirit.

ON THE RECORD

It's a New Day—Use It or Lose It

This is the beginning of a new day. God has given it to me to use as I will. I can waste it or use it for good, but what I do today is important because I am exchanging a day of my life for it. When tomorrow comes, this day will be gone forever, leaving in its place something I have traded for it. I want it to be gain and not loss. I want it to be good and not evil.

Dr. Hartsill Wilson

What a wonderful approach to life, and what a wonderful witness for our Lord!

Of course, Judge Fay has bad days. Much of his work is frustrating and lonely. Over the years he has tried some of the most heinous criminal cases, but he never allows himself to get down. He sees the worst of life in his judicial deliberations, yet he never lets it overwhelm him. Rather, he starts each day with an optimistic view. "When I was growing up," Pete recalls, "I was surrounded by optimists. My parents had nothing, but they did have optimism — and it was contagious."

Over and over again, Pete has reminded me of the uplifting power of our faith. If we truly accept the teachings of Jesus, we can't help but become infected with an abiding optimism to help carry us through the traumas of life, regardless of the circumstances. Pete doesn't carry his Bible everywhere, and I don't think he tries to "convert" anyone. He has simply allowed his faith to influence the way he treats others, and most of the time that's all any of us have to do.

How can others possibly know the power of faith if they never see it in your life? How can they believe what *you* believe if you violate by your actions the life-giving message of the gospel? Putting faith into practice is not just God's gift to us. It encompasses our responsibility to Him because it's His priority for us.

Perhaps you have it all together on Saturday or Sunday after celebrating God's grace and love in church. You have given thanks for your many blessings. You have prayed for family and friends. You have asked God's help for the needy, the grieving, the sick and wounded. And you have uplifted in prayer the needs of others and asked God to meet your own.

That's the easy part.

Then Monday comes along. Our priorities and focus seem to change. The peace of our prayerful Sunday traditions fades into the secular, competitive realties of life. We become rude and unforgiving. Instead of lifting up, we tear down and discourage those in need. Your neighbors probably see you leaving for church, perhaps carrying your Bible and looking pretty religious in a suit. Imagine what must be going through their minds when on Monday you barely wave as you head off to work. It's often the little things that tarnish our image as followers of Christ.

Many years ago I began a spiritual discipline that has helped me rise above the annoyances of everyday life and cast a bright outlook for others. It's pretty simple, but I challenge you to try it: the first thing you do when you wake up in the morning is to thank God for all the blessings in your life. It may not seem like much, but it changes your whole perspective for the day. If the coffee is a little weak or the newspaper hasn't arrived on time, you can still smile and enjoy life because you have reminded yourself that God blesses you beyond your expectations. It keeps those minor irritants in perspective.

It is mostly a matter of how you look at life. If you wake up believing it will be a lousy day, your negative predictions are likely to come true. On the other hand, if you get up with a happy heart and a positive spirit, things inevitably will be better. There are always reasons to be hopeful, reasons to be uplifted, and reasons to have faith, especially when you start the day in prayer — thanking God for the blessings of each day.

Rediscovering our faith means learning anew how to see the best in life even as the worst cries out for our attention. People of faith do not necessarily have it better than others, just the ability to see things that others do not see. It is that spirit we need to share.

A great example of this is the way Jesus looked beyond the surface and saw things that others missed. His followers came to Him in a panic and said, "Five thousand people showed up to hear You speak, and they're hungry and we don't have any food." Jesus said, "We've got some bread and fish, don't we?"

A blind man cried out to Jesus, and His followers tried to chase him away. But Jesus told them to go back and get him because He saw an opportunity for something good to happen. And it did! A crowd of religious people were about to stone a woman who had cheated on her husband, but Jesus saw the inner beauty of the woman and defended her.

I saw this spirit lived out in courageous ways by Captain Harry Jenkins, who flew combat missions over Hanoi during the Vietnam War. One day when he was about to drop his payload, a barrage of antiaircraft fire slammed into his plane, forcing him to bail out into an uncertain captivity. For the next seven years he was tortured and nearly starved to death.

Harry's captors had one goal: break his spirit. But Harry decided early on that the only way he would survive the hellish Vietnamese prison system was to focus on what little good he could find, transforming his environment through sheer will and his strong Christian faith.

Instead of cursing the rats that entered his cell, he befriended them and decided to enjoy their antics. Bare walls became fantasy movie screens as he recreated scenes from popular films. If he noticed his fellow prisoners becoming despondent or depressed, he got them laughing with his jokes. Even amid the horrible conditions of the infamous "Hanoi Hilton," Harry always found some good news to relay to his buddies, and when there really wasn't any good news, he made some up. The anchor of it all was his strong faith in God and the knowledge that He was at his side even as he was being brutally tortured by a ruthless enemy. God gave Harry a sense of humor, but better yet, He empowered Harry with love that radiated through a contagious sense of humor.

A core group of POW believers had dug deep to recollect from memory some of their favorite Scripture passages and hymns. They pooled their recollections, and before long, most of the captured men could quote from more than 120 hymns and passages from the Bible. "Without our faith in God, we could not have made it," one of Harry's cellmates told me shortly after the prisoners of war were set free.

Harry didn't lecture on survival tactics or preach a sermon about perseverance. He lived it out, and his perseverance saved his fellow prisoners from despair and death. He practiced the power of looking for the good signs in life — which he called God's blessings — and it enabled him to rise above his horrible circumstances. And he forgave his enemies.

To this day, more than thirty years after their release from prison, Harry's buddies contend they are alive because of him.

Unlike Captain Jenkins, some people who are considered to be quite religious are often the last people to see the good that surrounds them. In fact, religious people are sometimes the first to point out how awful things are.

A friend of mine told me about an acquaintance of his who decided, after an absence of several years, to start going to church again. The two met later, and my friend asked how he liked the church service. "The music was nice, but then the preacher screamed at us for about forty-five minutes about how awful the world is and how it won't be getting any better. Now I remember why I quit going to church in the first place."

How sad! I understand the preacher's desire to remind people that our earthly home is temporary, so we shouldn't get too attached to it. But what a shame that a spiritual leader would be characterized as screaming about how awful things are. Has the man never seen a sunset or held a granddaughter or enjoyed a good meal? Sure, we live in very difficult and even dangerous times. The security alert colors are nothing to sneeze at, for at any time we could experience an event equivalent to the horrors of 9/11. But why focus on that when flowers still bloom, when children smile? Why not look for something to celebrate, even as we mourn the reality of living in a fallen world?

> **ON THE RECORD**
>
> **Don't Wait for Opportunity**
>
> *I was brought up to not be afraid of hard work. Don't wait for opportunity to knock. Go find it. Make sure your dreams are really what you want, and then set up a plan to get there.*
>
> **Kirk Jenkins**
> **Commercial real estate broker,**
> **Scottsdale, Arizona**

Attitudes show through instantly. You know the clues. Positive thoughts reflect praise, cheer, a warm smile, optimism, hope, and concern for others. Sour people — and sadly we confront them all too often in life — complain, criticize, gossip, and worry and are frustrated, hurt, discouraged, and lonely. Any of these latter moods can become huge turnoffs to those looking for God's love through your life.

It's right about here when someone usually says something like, "That's easy for you to say, Mr. Ambassador, former big-city newspaper publisher, friend of presidents and corporate moguls." Some would say I have had an easy go of things — but actually that is not the case.

If ever there was a time in my life when I needed God's presence, it was when, at age thirteen, I moved into that rough section of Queens, New York. My parents had split up, I had just started high school, and I was working to help supplement my mother's modest income so we could pay the bills. Back then, "divorce" was a dirty word, something most people whispered about. The fact that my parents were separating was shameful and embarrassing; I kept the news to myself. All I knew was that our predicament was bad and that things would likely get worse. And they did.

We had very little money then, and only a glimmer of hope. But somehow I just knew we would get by. Through those tough times I learned how to recalibrate my inner spirit and the power of faith to lift me up. I quickly came to one simple conclusion: I wanted OUT. Forget that things looked grim. Never mind that we were broke and that a college education seemed totally out of reach. Never mind that there seemed to be few options available.

I learned in that traumatic and frightening experience that even a little hope can become a powerful resource. One tiny bit of encouragement, one small success, could become a huge miracle. In some ways I think I was one of the lucky ones. As I struggled to get ahead, there just wasn't time to feel sorry for myself. We knew that the trick for success would be to make the best of even the smallest opportunity. No matter how often I felt like giving up, I knew that if I could do well in high school, I just might be able to make it through college.

Deep in my heart, I felt I could beat the odds. All I had to do was look around me to see what happened to those who gave up, and that motivated me to keep going. I saw so many others who felt sorry for themselves, and I think their hopelessness must have scared me into action. If I wasn't going to make it, at least I would go down swinging.

For one of the first times in my life, I prayed. I prayed for good grades. I asked God to rescue me from my misery. I prayed for the means to get a college education so that I could earn a decent living. And above all, I asked God to lead me to someone who could become my partner for life, someone with whom I could create the loving, unified family I never had as a kid.

When your back is against the wall, you quickly discover that in life there is a choice: I could give up and accept this miserable fate, or I could fight my way out. For me there was only one choice. I would fight and I would find and nurture that God-given spirit within.

Despite my circumstances, others would describe me as a cheerful, smiling teenager. Perhaps my attitude was akin to whistling in the dark to overcome fear. I quickly learned that having a positive disposition conveys a potential for success, and it worked.

It is easy to understand why some people yield to bitterness and hatred when they face seemingly hopeless odds, but we need to remind them that it's their choice. Such people need help; they need mentors; they need encouragement. They need to know that they too have equal access to a faith that will carry them through anything.

What I needed was absolute determination that I could succeed. It started with hard work and a sense of inner confidence that I would prevail — even when deep down I wasn't sure. Failure was not an option. I simply had to pull my life together.

But it takes more than an optimistic attitude and big dreams to win. It takes faith in God to guide your way. Throughout the Bible, He promises us hope and the ability to endure tough times. When people let you down or try to tear you down, shake it off — and rejoice in the love of God. He can heal it all.

When the Berlin Wall went up, the East German Communists delighted in tossing garbage over the barrier. In contrast, the West Germans collected food and Bibles for the East Germans — and they prayed for their communist enemies. One side lived in despair; the other radiated hope and prayer. What a lesson for us!

Someone once told me that it is important to *look* successful. That means dressing well, so I went out and bought a cheap sports jacket from a wholesale house in lower Manhattan. The place was a dump, but the jacket looked great. I wore it often and, yes, my friend was right. That silly coat gave me a sense of inevitability that good things were coming. California Governor Arnold Schwarzenegger describes it this way: "To be successful you create a vision of what you want to be and then live into that picture as if it were already true." Whatever the approach, the goal is to tap the blessings given you by God in ways that honor His kingdom.

With God's help and that sports jacket, I was going to create my own fate. I was going to do everything humanly possible to generate a positive, can-do energy that would lead to success. I was going to win this battle. In essence I was *ordaining* myself to succeed. With the help of that inner spirit and prayer, good things could be achieved.

Have you ever wondered why some people are determined and optimistic? What gives them such a passionate commitment to be positive, to see life's potential rather than its problems? What makes them upbeat in the face of disaster? I believe the answer is simple: Each has recalibrated this spirit of inevitability. Psalm 51:10 says it well: "Renew a steadfast spirit within me."

If you are as fortunate as I have been, God has placed in your life people (like my high school math teacher) who help revive your inner spirit with the simple power of encouragement and concern. These are dependable friends who have an amazing ability to bring out the best in us. They empower our lives. They help us spark a spirit of self-confidence and optimism built on small increments of achievement. It is incredibly true, isn't it, how one small success begets another. Often our strength in one area generates success in an area where we are not so strong.

If you have experienced the loving hand of someone who is committed to your success, you are enormously blessed. You know the joy that comes from someone who reflects God's love and grace and causes you to know God, to trust Him, and to love Him.

Let's face it. You will never be free of disappointments, failures, tragedies, or unfairness. There are no gravy trains in life. Sometimes there isn't even any gravy — yet there are simple acts of encouragement to keep you going. A high school coach sends you into the game. A new friend takes you under his wings. A minister or rabbi consoles your broken heart. A teacher helps you through a tough course. A good deed, an encouraging word, an important lesson taught — these all convert a dim outlook into a bright future.

When someone slams the door in your face, do you give up, or do you know in your heart that the welcome mat is just around the corner? Do you worry about your problems, or are you confident you will solve them? Do you start the day making a mental list of all the things that are wrong about your life, or do you wake up counting your blessings?

To tell the truth, I was in way over my head for most of the jobs I have had. But God knew this all along and forced me to stretch into the person He knew I could become. In reality we don't own anything — not our talents, not our resources, not our lives. We receive all as gifts from a loving God. We are simply stewards of God's blessings to us for a brief time. In the end we are accountable to Him for those resources. He is the owner; we are merely the trustees. We are well fed by that loving God, and the question we must always answer is, what are we doing for *Him*?

Take time right now to put down this book and get out a notepad and pencil. Using the checklist that follows, rediscover the God-provided blessings of your life. Focus on the positive aspects of the world around you. Reflect on the great things that have come your way. Think about the ones you didn't even deserve. Recall those that came about despite your unwillingness to accept them. Make a list and reflect on it. Share it with your family and close friends. You will be amazed at how many blessings you really have. One thought will remind you of another. This exercise will bring you great joy.

Keep your pad handy. Add to your notes as the days and weeks go by. You will be reminded of dozens of amazing blessings in your life, and perhaps you will rediscover how many blessings you have to share with others. When the blessings of your life are tallied, you will begin to rediscover your true inner spirit. God wants you to make something special of your life. In so doing, you will help make the world a better place.

I have found that such discipline helps me maintain the habit of looking for the best in myself and in others. Life seems more promising, problems less threatening, and success more achievable.

As you recalibrate your life and purpose, it is important to sense God's hand in your work. It is also critical to remember Paul's admonition that we must "prepare God's people for works of service" (Ephesians 4:12).

Radiating God's love and purpose for you is a full-time job.

FAITH KEEPERS

Rediscover the Blessings of Life

- Name five mentors who changed your life, and list the reasons why.
- Name three teachers who inspired your best in school or college.
- Name your best friends. What's special about each one?
- Name five accomplishments that you care most about.
- Name five uplifting personal values that you hope others would use to describe you.
- Name five people who have helped you in the past month.
- Name five people you would like to help next month.

Recalibrating My Purpose

- What do I want out of life?
- How do I want to be remembered by family and friends?
- Do I have the ability to move on after defeat and disappointment?
- Have I comforted someone who is hurting or sick?
- Have I uplifted an underappreciated associate at work or a friendly clerk at the store?
- How often do I list all the good things in my life for which I should be enormously grateful?
- Do I tell my family how much I love them?
- Do I seek to renew contact with long-lost friends?
- Do I praise a good deed or do something to make a new friend?
- Do I thank God for His many blessings?

Chapter 5

FACE PROBLEMS WITH HOPE

You Can't Quit

There is a power beyond man — Divine Providence, the will of God. It is a powerful source of strength if you can get in tune with it. . . .

Some people look upon any setback as the end. They're always looking for the benediction rather than the invocation. . . .

Most of us have enough problems so that almost any day we could fold up and say: "I've had it." But you can't quit.

Vice President Hubert Humphrey

God's Comfort

What a wonderful God we have — he is the Father of our Lord Jesus Christ, the source of every mercy, and the one who so wonderfully comforts and strengthens us in our hardships and trials. And why does he do this? So that when others are troubled, needing our sympathy and encouragement, we can pass on to them this same help and comfort God has given us.

2 Corinthians 1:3 – 4 TLB

Trusting in Him

When we put our hope in Him, it is then that we begin to know a bedrock sense of safety, stability, and sanity regardless of the chaos. Trusting in Him is the front edge of the healing that our hearts so long for.

Joe Stowell, teaching pastor, Harvest Bible Chapel, Illinois

Nobody likes to hang around a naysayer, the guy who always weighs in with the negatives. We used to call these people "contrarians." Comment on the beautiful blue sky and they'll respond, "But it's supposed to rain tonight." Share your plans for a vacation at the beach and all they can comment on is sunburns and sand. They are probably not as discontent as they sound, but they don't appear to be people you'd want to party with.

In this chapter we will consider what happens when Christians become known for their pessimism. Remember, this is a book about having a faith that attracts rather than repels people. My premise in this chapter is that even if your beliefs are not shared by those around you, they will respect you and be drawn to you if you avoid a negativism about life today. U.S. Senator Hubert Humphrey was a great example of how this works.

In terms of political philosophy, Senator Humphrey and I disagreed on many issues. Yet, as often as we were on opposite sides, I never ceased to admire his determination and faith. Even after his defeat in a close election for president in 1968, he refused to feel defeated. You simply knew that his life, exuding energy and optimism, was grounded in faith, and that the cornerstone of his faith was a loving God.

Senator Humphrey would never, ever quit, not even in the final campaign of his life, a losing battle against cancer in which he

ON THE RECORD

From Darkness to Light

Darkness is real, and it can be terrifying. Sometimes it seems to be everywhere. So the question for us is, what do we do when darkness surrounds us? St. Paul answered that question. He said we must walk as children of light. President Reagan taught us that this is our mission, both as individuals and as a nation.

Rev. John Danforth
At the memorial service
for Ronald Reagan

knew the odds were solidly against him. He never doubted that he could win that fight. Each day was a blessing to be cheerfully enjoyed to the fullest. He dismissed bad days when he felt terrible and looked forward to the good ones. He had a tremendous will to hang on in tough times, and he did. He never had any bitterness.

Somehow Senator Humphrey always managed to turn bad news into good. In one of his most impassioned and final speeches from the floor of the Senate, he reminded his colleagues and all of us that "adversity is an experience, not a final act. My faith and hope get me from day to day."

Such energy, enabling us to overcome overwhelming adversity, comes from an inner spirit that is fueled by determination, resilience, and faith in God. Somehow those who suffer manage to prevail by dealing head-on with tragedy and despair. In the process, they turn their enemies into friends. That is why it is so important to avoid the gloom and despair that often characterize us. I am convinced that it is not our Christian beliefs that turn others off, but our negative attitudes.

There is comfort in knowing that by putting aside the bad breaks we open new possibilities for living life to the fullest — through its peaks and valleys. As Paul told the people of Corinth, "When I am weak, then I am strong" (2 Corinthians 12:10).

Hubert Humphrey reminded us that there is always someone there who wants to help, who hasn't tossed in the towel. Even when heavy debts forced his father to sell the family farm, Humphrey

ON THE RECORD

Dealing with Tragedy

Every generation is faced with unexpected tragedy that challenges us to galvanize our beliefs and priorities in the face of great difficulty. Only by remaining resolute in the face of such hardship can we hope to see beyond the emotion and anger and learn the valuable lessons that lie at the heart of each of life's experiences.

Rachel Yould
Rhodes scholar and *USA Today* honoree

believed that life isn't what you've lost, but what you have left. What a wonderful approach to dealing with the inevitable setbacks in life!

God sometimes places us in times of uncertainty and failure. He expects us to grow from the experience and to appreciate His grace. Even in these times of failure and disappointment we must have an outward focus. We need to turn away from the selfishness of our lives and look outward to others. In doing so we are reminded that others struggle, that others have far greater needs than we. Paul reminds us,

> And we know that in all things God works for the good of those who love him, who have been called according to his purpose (Romans 8:28).

It is that abiding faith and refusal to give up that gave a young paraplegic a platform to spread God's message of grace worldwide. As a teenager, Joni Eareckson suffered a spinal cord injury that left her paralyzed from the neck down. Initially she experienced all the usual emotions of despair and depression, but one day she made the decision to use whatever strength and ability she had to bring joy to others. She learned to draw by placing a paintbrush in her mouth. She discovered her beautiful voice could still sing the hope-filled hymns of the church. Soon she was in demand all over the world — often before stadium audiences in Billy Graham crusades — sharing her inspiring story with millions.

Joni had to make a choice while in the hospital. She could continue feeding her anger and depression, complaining to God for allowing her injury to happen. Or she could accept her condition as a gift that would allow her to brighten the lives of others.

Aren't you glad she chose the latter?

The mid-1600s were the worst of times in England. The Anglican Church was in trouble, Puritans were being persecuted, and Charles I was on trial for treason. There was famine, the economy was in terrible shape, and the country was headed toward civil war. Despite such dire straits, Sir Robert Shirley Baranett chose to build a new church. The inscription on that church today says it all:

Built by those who did the best of things in the worst of times. We all can do the best of things in the worst of times.

So can you.

Since September 11, 2001, and the wars in Afghanistan and Iraq that followed, we have been overwhelmed by reminders that the soul of America is strong. Our country has rallied in ways almost never dreamed imaginable. Family members have survived unbelievable trauma and loss by moving forward one day at a time. We are a resilient nation, and the rest of the world has learned again and again that adversity strengthens us.

For many of us, our families and friends have become even more precious. We appreciate as never before every breath of air, every bit of food, every loving hug. We had taken so much for granted, hadn't we?

ON THE RECORD

Judged by Adversity

Men are judged not only by their achievements and successes. They are judged by how they handle adversity.

Dean Rusk
Secretary of state during the war in Vietnam

Embedded in many of us is the conviction that nothing can destroy the human spirit. Even when life throws us a terrible curve, we manage to find reason to hope. In the end, hardship helps us discover that inner strength, and it gives us the courage to move on, to grow, and to learn from the experience, no matter how tough.

What about you? What drags you down? Who bugs you and why? What can you do to move beyond a broken relationship or to restore it? If you get up in the morning hating your job, what can you do to change it? If you are constantly broke, how can you better manage your resources? In summary, what can you do to turn your bad news into good?

I often take the train from San Diego to downtown Los Angeles for board meetings. It is a convenient alternative for avoiding freeway traffic jams, and it's a wonderful way to start the day. The trip is spectacular, much of it running close to the beach near the route where Father Junipero Serra more than two hundred years ago founded a series of twenty-one California missions extending from San Diego to north of San Francisco. The scenery is spectacular: hillsides covered with beautiful wildflowers, surfers riding huge waves, U.S. Marines on training exercises, and tourists walking the pristine beaches. How can life be anything but good at such times?

On one trip my attention was drawn to loud comments by a very unhappy man seated several rows behind me. It was a perfect, sunny morning — for everyone but this bitter old man. Absolutely nothing was right. The weather was terrible, the train was late, the conductor was rude, the free orange juice was sour, and the seats were uncomfortable. Then he picked up his free copy of the morning newspaper and took off again, spewing yet another avalanche of pessimism about what he read. It was only eight in the morning, and he had poisoned the world around him.

Are you attracted to people like that? Of course not. None of us are. This man reminded me of the cynical waitress in the book *Travels with Charley* by John Steinbeck:

The dame was one of those people who can suck pleasure dry and get no sustenance from it. Such people spread a grayness in the air above them.... She got me. I felt so blue and miserable I wanted to crawl into a plastic cover and die.

How often do we let the problems we see in society drag us into an attitude of complaining and criticism? I'm sure you don't think of yourself as a grouch, but how do others see you? Do they see someone who faces the legitimate problems in life with a spirit of fear and negativity or with an attitude of hope that comes from knowing that God has everything in control?

Life is full of bad news, long faces, and heavy hearts, but they don't need to bring us down. When you allow failure and tragedy to become permanent conditions, you choke out any chance for personal recovery. Success sometimes has its roots in the lessons of defeat. You lose a race and then train harder and win. You flunk a test, study your heart out, and — on the third try — finally make the honor roll. You are passed over for a raise, tune up your performance, and the next time around land the promotion you wanted. As a friend once told me, failure is the opportunity to begin again — only more intelligently.

Romans 5:3–5 puts it well:

> We also rejoice in our sufferings, because we know that suffering produces perseverance; perseverance, character; character, hope. And hope does not disappoint us, because God has

ON THE RECORD

Perseverance

Perseverance has carried me through the most discouraging times of my life [loss of husband]. I have learned that bad things happen to everyone — regardless of the goodness of the life you lead. If you persevere, however, you can turn your pain and sense of failure into something rewarding.

**Stephanie Bartlett
Teacher and *USA Today* honoree,
North Carolina**

poured out his love into our hearts by the Holy Spirit, whom he has given us.

Although I never really look forward to problems, I have learned that we are at our best when we are being tested and face adversity. The process helps us examine our character, set priorities, and learn from our failures. We learn from pain; it forces us back to basics and hones our ability to cope. It also reminds us that our Lord is always there, even in the darkest moments.

My daughter recently taught fourth graders who have come from some pretty desperate situations. Life for many of her students was nothing but bad news. The only hope many of these kids experienced was found in the classroom. Each fall, just before Thanksgiving, Carrie passed out to each child a list of all the students in the class, with a blank space by each name. By each name students were asked to write something special in the spirit of Thanksgiving about their classmates. A word of encouragement. A compliment. A reason they liked them.

The results were then grouped by student and redistributed in such a way that no one could identify the author of each positive comment. The kids were dumbfounded. For many, it was the first time they had ever been praised. Most had never been told they were winners. At the end of the day, one young boy came up to Carrie in tears, sobbing, "Mrs. Hasler, no one has ever, ever told me I was any good at anything."

How sad! — but what a powerful message about the importance of an encouraging word. Who are the people in your life who need to be told they are good at something? What would happen if you made it a point to speak a word of encouragement every time you

ON THE RECORD

Living to the Fullest
I will be faithful, fruitful,
and cheerful to the end.

A person just told he had terminal cancer with three months to live

bumped into one of these "students" of yours? As Christian ambassadors, it really is our privilege to demonstrate God's love through the power of our personal example and demeanor.

During my years in the Pentagon, we had no choice but to persevere, to pick up the pieces left by those who preceded us, and to somehow try to end the war in Vietnam. I confess that there were days when we thought the situation was hopeless; with so much of the public opinion against us, it was hard to stay positive. I can only credit my strong faith in God for helping me push ahead beyond the bad news that came in every day. Haven't you had moments like that? Haven't you had to ask God for strength to help keep you going on those days when everything seems to go wrong? That is when we need the strength James writes about in his letter:

> Blessed is the man who perseveres under trial, because when he has stood the test, he will receive the crown of life that God has promised to those who love him (James 1:12).

One of my responsibilities in the Defense Department back then was to develop a plan for obtaining humane treatment for our prisoners of war and missing men in the war. By 1969 more than 5,000 servicemen were listed either as prisoners of war or as missing in action, and we knew that some were dying in captivity. Virtually all were held in total isolation. Food was in short supply, and severe torture was common. Some were critically ill and needed immediate medical attention. Meanwhile, the families of these men needed hope, and it was our duty to give them some — no matter how tough the situation.

In May 1969, Secretary Laird and I revealed at a nationally televised Pentagon news conference the horrible conditions under which our men were being held. We cited known cases of Americans who had been seriously wounded but denied medical attention, and we released photos proving that our men were being systematically tortured. One involved a picture of now – U.S. Senator John McCain, who had been shot down over Hanoi, broke many bones in the bailout, and suffered from all of them being rebroken as a form of torture after his capture.

So that the POW/MIA families would better understand the import of our public campaign in behalf of their loved ones, I led a team of military briefers to some fifty military installations across the country. We met personally with some 3,000 relatives who were mad and frustrated. Some were understandably bitter and deeply traumatized, close to the breaking point. All wanted answers — now.

Somehow in all this mess, I needed to convey a sense of hope, even when deep down I wondered where I could find it. In our briefings we struggled to give even the slightest glimmer of optimism. Our arguments were only minimally reassuring. During these times, the only thing that brought hope was my faith in God, and I did my best to convey that to the families who had nearly lost all hope.

When the POWs were finally released, we all found huge inspiration from their extraordinary patriotism and bravery. Seldom has there been a more dramatic or convincing proof of the power of the inner spirit than the dozens of incredible stories they told after they were released. They had been courageous beyond belief, and they were kept alive by an abiding faith in God. Each night, through an amazing tap code, they passed along prayers by tapping them through the prison walls, ending each with the simple encoded message that spelled GBU: "God bless you."

Three letters, shared once a day, was all the hope these men had — and it sustained them for months at a time. Talk about a group of people who had a right to complain! But they knew that despite their circumstances, God was at work in the way He sustained them during their suffering.

It is because of stories like this that I have a hard time when I hear people complain about things that seem small by comparison. And it seems as if we Christians are doing an awful lot of that lately. Look at how we complain about church, even though we are blessed to live at a time in history when church attendance is at an all-time high and the church seems to be thriving. And sadly, our complaining has led to far too many church splits and pastors quitting because they just can't deal with stress and change. Is it any wonder that those outside the family of God are not eager to join us? We have so much to offer the world — so much hope and joy and excitement — but too often we portray an image that is anything but exciting.

I am convinced we have the most exciting story of all to *tell* as well as to *live*. If we could only get beyond the pessimism that seems to be second nature for many of us.

I recall a stirring scene at the 1992 Summer Olympic Games, when I was ambassador to Spain. More than 100,000 spectators jammed the Monjuic Olympic Stadium for the 400-meter track finals, where Derek Redmond, a star athlete from Great Britain, was expected to set a world record. My family and I had some of the best seats in the house — just ten rows from the track and alongside

ON THE RECORD

Uplifting Others

Do not let any unwholesome talk come out of your mouths, but only what is helpful for building others up according to their needs.
Ephesians 4:29

the royal box where King Juan Carlos, Queen Sofia, and their family had gathered. We had a perfect view of the finish line.

The runners lined up, the starting gun sounded, and the race was on. Within a second or two, Derek was well into the lead on his way to a gold medal. The cheers were deafening as the runners approached the finish line. Then something went terribly wrong. With about fifty meters to go, Derek Redmond collapsed on the track, screaming in pain. He had torn his hamstring.

In a split second, a man in front of me jumped from his seat, leaped over the barrier that separated us from the track, and ran to the athlete. Without any hesitation, he picked Redmond up, threw the runner's arm over his shoulder, and dragged the athlete toward the finish line. Just before the finish, the man let go, and Derek hobbled across the line on his own. The man was Derek's father, and he was determined that his son would finish the race. Together this father and son had produced one of the most spectacular Olympic finishes in history.

Derek Redmond did not set a world record that day. He did something infinitely more important: he showed us how to win the race of life. The Olympic run was not a failed race. He had ended it with determination and raw courage. He simply moved on. No self-pity. No remorse. No giving up.

It was Eric Liddell all over again. That Christian, celebrated in the film *Chariots of Fire*, drew his inspiration for winning the 400-meter run in the 1924 Olympics from Hebrews 12:1:

> Let us run with patience the race that is set before us,
> Looking unto Jesus the author and finisher of our faith (KJV).

Why do stories like this inspire us? Because they give us hope that we too can overcome the obstacles that lie before us. But more than that, we are drawn to people who do not let their bad experience get them down. There is something infectious about their spirit. And we desire to share in it somehow, to learn what it is that keeps them going when someone else might give up.

This is what I believe Jesus meant when He told us we are "the light of the world" (Matthew 5:14). It was His desire to see His followers be the ones who inspire others with their attitude of hope and joy, for He knew that would be the best way to bring others into His kingdom. I find it interesting that He never really laid out a plan to evangelize the world, but repeatedly called His followers to live in such a way that others would notice and become attracted to them.

Your life can have the same effect on others. We do not need to have a dramatic story like a prisoner of war or an Olympic athlete. All we need is to avoid the pessimism that so easily creeps into our lives and instead become a part of the solution rather than just complaining.

God often chooses to use the small things of life, the opportunities we often overlook, as powerful resources in our service to Him. Bestselling author Richard Carlson once admonished the world not to "sweat the small stuff" of life. Well, for the most part, life is small stuff, and God wants us to use it for His purpose.

God has created you, with the miracle of your uniqueness. In that creation He has given each of us different skills, different personalities to radiate His love — through our natural enthusiasm, our quiet example, our instincts, our contemplative nature, our conviction. Our personal example and demeanor can radiate the only Bible many people will ever see. It's important to reflect God's love in all we do — sometimes it even takes words. It's a huge responsibility, and if we leave it unattended, we become miserable hypocrites.

We are here not by chance, but rather by God's choosing. He has put us here at this place, at this time, to fulfill His special purpose for us and for our generation. One day. One person. One small deed at a time. This means being available and approachable, and it means trying to do the right thing all the time, even when you think no one is watching.

It takes an optimistic spirit, even when there is little to be optimistic about.

FAITH KEEPERS

How to Overcome Bad News

- Talk about your hurts and sorrow with friends.
- Remind yourself that you are never alone in dealing with sadness, anger, or fear.
- Don't take all the blame. Nothing in life occurs in a vacuum.
- Don't allow yourself to be discouraged.
- Remember that there is often a fine line between success and failure.
- Look beyond your mistakes and your pain. It's over. Move on.
- Develop a plan for picking up the pieces. Make sure it has a chance to work.
- Fix one small problem and move on to the next.
- Keep yourself strong — physically, mentally, emotionally, and spiritually.
- Laugh at yourself and the world around you. A sense of humor is great medicine.
- Don't sweat the small stuff.
- Focus on the big picture: family and friends and God's love.

How to Encourage the Discouraged

- Be compassionate, unselfish, and loving.
- Seek out opportunities to help others.
- Count your blessings.
- Pray *for* others and *with* others.
- Find the good in others.
- Celebrate the success of others as if it were your own.
- Forget your mistakes and move on.
- Help stamp out cynicism around you.
- Forgive and forget.
- Listen and observe.
- Acknowledge good deeds.
- Take advantage of what you have and erase thoughts of what might have been.
- Always be counted upon.
- Wear a cheerful countenance.
- Be strong and let nothing disturb your peace with God.

Adapted from *Finish Strong*

Chapter 6

SENSE THE HAND OF GOD

DRIVEN BY LOVE

Virtually every day I ask myself what my dad would have done. He was driven his entire life and in all instances by truly altruistic love for his fellow man. He never acted out of self-interest. And nothing was more important to him than God, family, and other people.

Taylor Batten, newspaper editor, Charlotte, North Carolina

BIGGER THAN LIFE

My dad was always bigger than life to me. He was (and still is) my hero. He was very patriotic but not a flag-waver. He was deeply religious but wouldn't grab your collar and preach. He had a sense of right and wrong that was unshakable. Integrity and honesty were a given, and his word or handshake was better than any contract.

Chris Jenkins, Covina, California

SOUND ADVICE

My mother gave us profound advice:
— Be honest and tell the truth.
— Be kind and care for the other guy.
— Don't look down on anyone.
— You have an obligation to help others.
— Compete hard, play to win. Be a good winner and a good loser too.
— Give the other guy credit and don't be a braggadocio.

President George H. W. Bush

You may think, from what you have read so far, that I'm a pretty lucky guy. Let me tell you, there's not enough luck in this world to have given me the great experiences I have had. In this chapter I want to encourage you to banish the word *luck* from your vocabulary and focus instead on how God is at work in your life. Whatever good has happened to you is not the result of luck or fate, but is a gift given directly by God (James 1:17). Nothing will draw you closer to the heart of God than accepting this profound truth.

Think back on the important crossroads of your life and reflect on how God provided for you. For me, one of the most evident provisions of God happened only a few days after being introduced at a wedding reception to a beautiful college senior. Months earlier, I had moved to San Diego, knew only a handful of people, and was barely off the ground with what would become a thirty-year career in the newspaper business. Frankly, I was too broke at the time to think seriously of marriage, but that didn't matter any — there were no candidates in the wings.

Joan and I had only a brief conversation at the reception, but she registered in my mind big-time. Maybe it was the spectacular red dress she wore or the warm way in which she greeted everyone she met. The next day I called for a date, but she told me she had other commitments. I almost dropped the idea of pursuing her, yet something told me I needed to persist. I did — and she turned me down a second time. Finally, on the third call, I convinced her to take a chance, and it changed our lives forever. Years later, she confessed that my

ON THE RECORD

Doing the Right Thing

Sometimes it helps you make the right decision when you step back and think how someone you respect very highly would have acted if presented with the same decision.

Floyd Fales
Financial analyst,
Atlanta, Georgia

invitations had been turned down because she thought I was far too old. At the time, she was twenty and I was twenty-six.

Soon after we met, Joan left for her senior year at Stanford. On the morning of her departure for the fall semester, she invited me to her home for breakfast with her parents. They assumed, of course, that something was up. After our good-byes, I returned to my small apartment to sort it all out. It was there that morning that I sensed something powerful at work in my life. Later I came to appreciate that it was the hand of God. He had brought us together and had convinced me to persist. Yes, I felt like the luckiest guy in the world, but it went much deeper than that. I realized that God was at work in my life and was about to give me a partner to share the adventure.

Joan and I talked by phone every day until I was able to fly north for a weekend to meet her on campus. That Sunday we attended church at the university chapel, and an hour later — only a month after we had met for the first time — I asked her to marry me. All of this just weeks after first meeting her. Crazy? You bet! But it was also clear to both of us that God had planned this all along. For years we told our kids never, ever to do something so stupid, and in general, I would still counsel young people to avoid such a hasty courtship. At the same time, if it is clear that God is leading you, you have no choice but to follow.

ON THE RECORD

The Power of Your Shadow
You can't be a beacon
if your light don't shine.
Old country western song

Too often we take for granted these marvelous provisions of God in our lives. I believe that one reason so many Christian marriages have lost their passion is that couples forget that their relationship is "ordained." Imagine — the Creator of the universe brought you and your spouse together. Do you thank God every day for your husband or wife? Do the two of you remind each other that your love comes from God? When you make the effort to sense God's presence in your life, you are in effect deepening your relationship with Him. To take time out for reflection, for counting your blessings, is important to this process.

ON THE RECORD

Learning Early

I teach my first-graders to think about others and to treat others with kindness. I want them to grow up to be kindhearted, generous individuals who won't turn a blind eye on problems in their families, communities, or nation.

Beth Whiteman
***USA Today* honoree, Albany, New York**

It is good for us to have a quiet refuge where we can experience God in a special way. It doesn't have to be a mountaintop cabin. It can be a park bench in the city or a rocking chair by the fireplace. But for our faith to grow and draw us closer to God, we need to be deliberate about seeking Him in a private, personal manner. In our busy and complex lives, we need to set aside times and places where there is peace and refreshment, where we can experience God's serenity.

Several years ago we built a log home high in the Rocky Mountains above Telluride, a delightful old mining town in southwest Colorado. Across from our log home was a huge National Forest Service preserve set aside to protect a large population of endangered elk. On many occasions I would hike there to an open area that provides a 360-degree view of the night sky from an elevation of 10,000 feet. To this day, my Colorado friends call this spot the "Capen Knoll." They know I have visited it so often that I must have staked my claim there.

On a clear night, unobstructed by city lights, those high country skies are jammed with millions of stars and planets, accented by shooting meteors and man-made satellites. According to *National Geographic*, we can see without a magnifying lens several thousand stars; a pair of binoculars will bring into view 50,000; with a simple two-inch telescope, several hundred thousand stars can be seen. And the current estimate is that our galaxy, the Milky Way, contains about 200 billion stars. Such numbers are beyond human comprehension, yet they are all God's perfect creation — and a wonderful backdrop for prayer and thanksgiving. I never left the Capen Knoll without an overwhelming sense of God's love and presence everywhere. Psalm 46 puts it this way:

> *God is our refuge and strength,*
> > *an ever-present help in trouble.*
> *Therefore we will not fear, though the earth give way*
> > *and the mountains fall into the heart of the sea....*
> *Be still, and know that I am God (vv. 1–2, 10).*

If you do not regularly seek out God's presence in a very personal and private manner, make it a point to begin today. In fact, set this book down right now and reflect on how God has blessed you. Think of other ways you can "program" similar periods of reflection into your life: a Sunday drive, prayer during a long cross-country flight, a hike in the woods, or a walk in the park. Some do their best reflecting while jogging or working out. Whatever works for you, these are important times to replenish your soul, to rediscover the awesome power of God. But that is only the beginning.

We are here for a purpose and that, simply stated, is to serve God and to radiate His love to others. He expects more from us than simply understanding and appreciating His hand in our lives. He wants — in fact, commands — us to extend His reach through our own personal witness to others.

As you think about how you might serve those around you, take a minute to think about how others — your own mentors in faith — led you to the Lord. Who encouraged you to pray and to read the Bible? Who helped you understand the inspiration and power of the Word? What specifically did they do to further your faith journey? What have you learned from them that you can apply in your relationships with others?

Tom Phillips, the former chairman and CEO of Raytheon, confided that he had difficulty talking openly about his faith but that God had denied him the comfort of keeping quiet. Even as head of a huge corporation with billions invested in defense contracts, he often was propelled into the personal problems of those around him. Some needed the hand of God in their lives, and Tom, in his own gentle manner, would describe his faith and how he came to know the Lord. As Tom puts it, "When you are called, you must witness, and only God knows how He will use your witness." Good advice.

Sometimes we are reluctant to share our faith even within our own family. I have yet to meet a dedicated Christian family that does not struggle with the lost sheep in their midst. It can be very painful, because we want so much for them to enjoy the peace we have found and yet it's hard to break the ice. But 1 Peter 3:15 challenges us to be up to the task: "Always be prepared to give an answer to everyone who asks you to give the reason for the hope that you have. But do this with gentleness and respect."

ON THE RECORD

It's All about Values

We try very hard to coach values within our overall team environment. Some people call it chemistry when really it is all about values.

Dick Vermeil
Professional football coach

As a writer I have an understandable desire to encourage friends to write down their innermost thoughts about God and His importance in their lives. Keep a file. Add to it when you are inspired to express your thoughts. Set it aside in a special file in your computer. Before long you will have a powerful story — your testimony — and it can be shared in quiet, private, nonthreatening ways with those seeking greater meaning in their lives.

You do not need exceptional writing skills. Just speak from the heart. Pour out your soul. Talk about your hopes and dreams, your successes and failures, and what you learned from each. Share your faith, your career, your experiences. Help others understand how the Lord came into your life. Tell about people who inspired you along the way and why.

Make this a running commentary, if you will. File it away for later use, adding and editing as your heart moves you. You will be amazed at the power and wonder of that story. Through it, you will help those you love the most find their way. It is very important to be a witness for the hope and faith you have.

ON THE RECORD

The Joy of a Sense of Humor

My parents taught me that a sense of humor is the balance wheel of life. Have you ever met a fanatic with a sense of humor?

Ruth Bell Graham

In Greek mythology, when Odysseus, the king of Ithaca, went off to war, he entrusted the education of his son, Telemachus, to the king's close friend, Mentor, whose job was to prepare the boy to be the next king. Mentor became Telemachus' constant companion, serving as counselor, advisor, encourager, and challenger. Mentor was a spectacular teacher and an inspiring role model — so much so that to this day we honor his achievement with the word *mentor* to describe a "wise and faithful counselor."

Mentors are very important, especially in developing our faith and our knowledge of the Word. You may have had many such mentors in your life. They cause you to leverage your energies and talents. They help you aspire to goals that seem far beyond your grasp. They mold your character and shape your standards of integrity. They uplift when you are down, and take you to task when you go off course. Some remain at your side for years; others touch your life for just a moment.

Such role models influence the direction of our faith and lives and careers. They remind us of our talents and passions and help us discover and nurture our inner spirit. They energize our lives, challenging us to take chances and to reach for the stars.

These are people whom you turn to when you are in trouble or have failed miserably. You laugh together, and cry too. You pick up the pieces with their encouragement. You seek their input on an important decision. You lean on them when you are discouraged and simply need to talk out a problem or vent a frustration. They are among the first people you call to report important family news, and above all, they are always there when you need them.

Who are your mentors? Perhaps it was an elementary school teacher, a high school coach, a parent, a trusted friend, someone at work, a pastor or church youth leader, a spouse or sibling, or a military officer.

Without someone to look up to, you might have lost it all. Writer James Michener puts it especially well:

> If you are lucky in life, you'll meet someone who will enlarge your horizon. Then you'll realize there's another world out there. If you don't, you are terribly unlucky — and may miss the whole ball game.

Mel Laird was one of those very special people who thrived on mentoring others. The list of those he has advised and cajoled along the way is amazing: a president of the United States (Gerald Ford, who was his soul mate in Congress for years), two secretaries of state (Larry Eagleburger and Colin Powell), dozens of congressmen and two U.S. senators (John Warner of Virginia and the late John Chaffee of Rhode Island), a comptroller general of the United States (Charles Bowsher), a national security advisor (Brent Scowcroft), a vice president of the United States (Dick Cheney), and one of the first blacks named a general in the U.S. Air Force (Chappie James). Mel was one of the most important mentors of my life too, and I still seek his counsel forty-five years after we met.

Another of my special mentors is Jim Lawrence, my deputy at the Pentagon. Jim, who was a highly decorated brigadier general in the Marine Corps, epitomizes the meaning of integrity and love of country. Because I was then, at age thirty-four, one of the youngest appointees in the Department of Defense, he provided a special maturity that helped temper my sometimes excessive exuberance. He led with conviction and courage, but also with a sense of modesty and humility. Above all, he was a patriot, prepared to die for his country. In 1950 he almost did.

During the Korean War, Major Jim Lawrence was forced to take command of what was left of a Marine battalion fighting to hold the Chosin Reservoir area, located in a rugged mountainous region just south of the border that divides China from North Korea. American intelligence had failed to discover 380,000 Chinese Communist regulars amassing along the border and preparing a sneak attack across the Yalu River against the American forces. The Marines were outnumbered ten to one. What started as an allied sweep turned into a treacherous battle for survival.

Jim's battalion commander became incoherent under the stress of the crisis and had to be relieved of command. Not long after, the deputy commander was severely wounded, and in that instant Major Jim Lawrence was left in command. By the end of the battle, his Marine battalion was decimated. Thousands were killed or wounded, and hundreds were victims of severe frostbite as temperatures plunged to 30 degrees below zero. One 3,200-man Army unit suffered 2,900 casualties. Heroically, Jim picked up the pieces and led his Marines to safety.

It was Jim Lawrence's quiet courage — and an abiding faith in God — that inspired his men to believe they could survive. When the war ended, Major Lawrence received the Navy Cross for heroism. The decoration ranks second only to the Medal of Honor.

God's love radiated around everything Jim Lawrence touched. "I learned from the example of a loving family that the Bible was the ultimate authority for living a useful and honorable life," he once told me. He believed passionately that the Golden Rule should be the Polaris for dealing with others and that, as he put it, "the teachings of Christ provide the best assurance for staying upright on the balance beam of life."

Many times we do not appreciate the role that mentors have played in our lives until years later, when, with the perspective of time and maturity, we better understand how much they influenced our development. When is the last time you told one of your mentors how special he or she has been to you? What a gift that would be. Send them an email. Pick up the phone. Write a thank-you note. Arrange a reunion. You will be amazed at how much joy you will bring to others in this process.

Now, before reading further, put the book down and take a few minutes to reflect on the memories of your mentors. What is special about them? Are you living up to what they taught you? Are you honoring them by mentoring others? Have you adequately thanked these special people for their advice and encouragement?

If you are fortunate, your most important mentors are your parents, or at least one of them. It is at home that we learn our most important lessons. It is in the comforting presence of loving parents that we share our hurts, our questions, and our hopes. Caring parents are always there, if for no other reason than to listen. They help bring stability and comfort in good times and bad. They help nurture our inner spirit so that their offspring are better equipped to face the real world.

ON THE RECORD

Uplift the Person at the Bottom

Do the best you can, no matter how insignificant it may seem at the time. No one knows more about solving a problem than the person at the bottom.

Sandra Day O'Connor
Retired U.S. Supreme Court justice

We asked young leaders through the *USA Today* leaders' survey what caused them to be successful. Most singled out at least one parent — a powerful reminder of the importance of family in understanding faith and the key priorities of life.

Effective families center their values on core principles that can be easily articulated and quickly understood. What Taylor Batten, an editor at the *Charlotte Observer*, had to say about his father was especially moving to me, because his father — Jim Batten — and I worked closely during my years with Knight Ridder. A highly respected leader in the newspaper business, Jim set the course, not just for his family but for all his media colleagues. Sadly, he died at age fifty-nine from a brain tumor.

"When my father died," Taylor told me, "we heard stories from dozens of people whose lives he had touched. His life demonstrated that the value of a life can be measured by the degree to which it improves the lives of others. He was a top corporate executive, but when he died, his titles and big office meant nothing."

Jim Batten was an inspiring mentor for his family and for hundreds of newspaper colleagues, including me.

Sadly, some people come along who teach us what *not* to do — but you can learn even from them. Such characters show us qualities we do not wish to possess; we neither admire them nor want to emulate their bad habits. Bosses who manage by fear and contribute to terrible job performance. Coaches who question your abilities and cause you to lose. Teachers who are boring and thus discourage academic pursuit. Friends who claim they will be there when you need them but aren't. Neighbors who always seem to see the worst in others.

Such cynics find fault with everything. They delight in dwelling on failure (particularly yours) and are unable to compliment success. They cut corners — often at your expense. With such negative attitudes they can have a devastating influence on your inner spirit. The trick is never to let such people poison your water and, instead, to get out from under the situation as fast as possible.

I will never forget one enormously unpopular Navy lieutenant commander who ruled my life when I served as a very junior officer on board a Pacific Fleet destroyer in the late 1950s. This officer was loaded with his own insecurities and seemed to enjoy ruling by fear. He micromanaged my every move, reminding me of my low rank and lack of experience. It was leadership by intimidation, and he got away with it. In the end, though, he did me a huge favor, because he taught me the importance of treating others with care and decency. It's a lesson I've never forgotten.

Ironically, that naval officer who taunted me at sea stopped by my Pentagon office twelve years later when he discovered that I was in the office of the secretary of defense. This was a whole new ball game for Ensign Capen. For openers, my Pentagon office was located near that of Secretary of Defense Mel Laird — which meant, in the pecking order of things military, I was in a very choice neighborhood.

ON THE RECORD

The Marriott Way

My father taught me to be results oriented and to never give up. My mother taught me compassion, love, and patience.

**J. W. "Bill" Marriott Jr.
Chairman and CEO,
Marriott International**

Power in Washington is measured in strange ways, so the size and location of your office often tell the world how much influence you have. My friends were impressed, but I didn't have the heart to tell them Laird wanted me close by so it would be easier and faster for him to chew me out — which he often did with great pleasure.

On that fateful morning, my secretary informed me that a friend from my destroyer days was outside my office waiting to "pay his respects." It was my naval nemesis. Respects? The officer who told me I would never amount to a hill of beans?

ON THE RECORD

Humble Service

Do nothing out of selfish ambition or vain conceit, but in humility consider others better than yourselves.

Philippians 2:3

That was one of those delicious moments we all dream about. The U.S. Constitution provides for civilian control over the military, so my equivalent rank as assistant to the secretary of defense was somewhere upwards of a three-star admiral or general. I let my destroyer colleague cool his heels in my outer office. Then I introduced him to my deputy, General Jim Lawrence, my highly decorated Marine Corps hero. It was a sweet victory.

I thanked the Navy commander for keeping me humble — and reminded myself what I had learned *not* to do when it came to leading others. I also thought of another piece of advice my mother once gave me: "Never burn your bridges, Dick." That made me wonder how the Navy commander, having done what he did, got back across the Potomac River that day.

When circumstances are unfairly tough, you quickly learn how to draw on our faith even as others hammer it. I learned another valuable lesson too. I've spent most of my career leading and managing large staffs. Some employees didn't make the grade. Even when we had to let people go, I would try to treat them with respect and dignity.

In times like that, it is particularly important to remember that we are all God's children and we are never the ultimate judge of anyone. The Lord has a way — usually just when we need it — of reminding us of our faults and failures, and He keeps us humble in the process. After all, we are imperfect humans with much to be humble about. One of my favorite stories makes the point:

A politician approached the check-in counter at Dulles International Airport and became obnoxiously impatient when he learned that his flight had been canceled. The senator pushed ahead of the line, slammed his ticket on the counter, and demanded another flight — with a first-class seat on the aisle.

The agent was calm and unimpressed as this pompous character shouted, "Do you know who I am?" The agent had no idea and couldn't care less, so he picked up the telephone, dialed into the airport public address system, and announced throughout the entire terminal: "Attention, all passengers. There is a person at gate 17 who does not know who he is. If anyone can help him, please report to gate 17 immediately."

So much for phony egos and undeserved self-importance.

Wherever you are in life, you have important opportunities to accept yourself as you are — faults and failures included. Our ultimate power comes when we acknowledge our human frailties. It is then that the Lord is strong in us and that His grace is made perfect in our weakness.

Jesus teaches us how to use problems to overcome fear and failure. He tells us, "Come to me, all you who are weary and burdened, and I will give you rest" (Matthew 11:28).

God's comfort also comes from radiating God's love through your personal example as a faithful mentor. Here are some ideas:

- Ask people to tell their story. You will be amazed at what you learn.

- Be a positive encourager. Everyone needs uplifting reinforcement.
- Be a patient, caring teacher.
- Be humble and modest. There is always someone else who can do it better.
- Don't flaunt authority. Use it with care and concern.
- Earn respect through strength of character and personal example.
- Be candid but gentle. Caring friends tell hard truths that help you do better.
- Set a moral tone and be principled.

I guarantee that after this exercise you will feel much better about yourself and the prospects ahead. And by mentoring others you will be saluting those who led you to a lifetime of faithful living.

All the prizes of life, all the praise you receive from others, all the trophies, medals, bank accounts, and fancy cars — these add up to nothing when balanced against the reassuring knowledge that you sense the hand of God and have helped extend it to those around you.

> Live such good lives among the pagans that, though they accuse you of doing wrong, they may see your good deeds and glorify God on the day he visits us (1 Peter 2:12).

FAITH KEEPERS

Sharing Your Faith

- Anchor your life to higher ground. Simply do the right thing.
- Conduct your personal life in an exemplary manner.
- Be a positive influence on one person a day.
- Center your life on principle, not popularity.
- When you make a mistake, admit it, apologize, and move on.
- Build trusting relationships, starting with your family and friends.
- Cherish your family and close friends. Never let them down.
- Be an encourager, especially to those without hope.
- Be optimistic, even when the world around you has collapsed.
- Serve others. When you do, you will be serving yourself.
- Live your life according to a higher calling — God's calling.

How to Reflect God's Optimism

- Optimists look for the good in others.
- Optimists are cheerful even when they can't be happy.
- Optimists seek a favorable twist to the world around them.
- Optimists laugh a lot. They laugh at themselves too.
- Optimists believe in the power of a smile. They always see good signs.
- Optimists love what they do, and they put all their heart into it.
- Optimists count their blessings. They feel good every day.
- Optimists learn to forgive.

- Optimists welcome new challenges. They take charge of their future.
- Optimists take chances. They dream. They are willing to stretch.
- Optimists refuse to surrender.
- Optimists do everything possible to avoid negative thoughts.
- Optimists tend to picture themselves doing something positive.
- Optimists have winning attitudes and big goals.

Adapted from *Finish Strong*

Chapter 7

HONE YOUR SPIRITUAL FITNESS

FINDING OUR MORAL COMPASS

We have watered down our moral standards, our expectations for honorable behavior and our sense of shame to the point that many of our youth are confused and have increasing difficulty locating either a moral compass or a worthy hero.

Former U.S. Senator Sam Nunn, Georgia

ASHES TO ASHES

Remember that when you leave this earth, you can take with you nothing that you have received — fading symbols of honor, trappings of power — but only what you have given: a full heart enriched by honest service, love, sacrifice, and courage.

Francis of Assisi

We have it all wrong. We think the South Beach Diet™ or plastic surgery, a new wardrobe or more money, or a lottery jackpot will bring us fulfillment. It won't. It will only make us thinner in outward appearance or better dressed or loaded with material excesses.

Jesus told us that if we want to gain, we must lose. That wasn't so much a call to be losers as a call to get rid of anything that is a distraction. Usually it means getting rid of burdensome attitudes or dependency on practically anything but God. As the Bible warns, you can't take it with you.

If you want to be truly empowered by your faith, you need to make sure it is "hardy" — a faith that is strong, not soft; vigorous, not wimpy. And in the same way that we periodically need to take stock of our physical health, so also with our spiritual health. We have to examine what truly matters in life and focus our time, talent, and energy on that. It is a process of trimming down, of dropping irrelevant distractions.

> ## ON THE RECORD
>
> ### God's Embrace
>
> *To value God is to embrace all of His teachings: to love your neighbor, to do justice, to practice mercy, and to walk humbly.*
>
> **Susan Cox-Stouffer**
> **Beavercreek, Ohio**

Most advice about improving your spiritual fitness centers around things like daily Bible reading, personal devotions, or an improved prayer life. Of course, these are extremely important. But from my vantage point, the best way to stay "spiritually fit" is to put your faith into action. Nothing strengthens your faith as much as reaching out to others.

Ryan was a freshman in high school when he noticed a kid from his class walking home with a huge pile of books in his arms. For some strange reason, as a friend told me, Kyle had emptied his school locker. To Ryan's horror, a bunch of older boys ran up and started to taunt Kyle, teasing him about his scrawny body, thick glasses, and bad case of acne.

Before long they had totally humiliated Kyle, tripping him, knocking him to the ground, and sending his glasses flying. The boy was in tears. It was a shameful attack. Ryan, upset at what he had witnessed, ran up to Kyle to help gather his books and then walked home with him. Out of the experience, Ryan and Kyle became good friends.

By the time Kyle became a senior he had outgrown those awkward early teenage years, gained confidence in himself, and become a class leader. Physically, he had filled out and was able to hold his own. Academically, he ranked at the top of his class and was asked to give the address at the commencement.

Kyle's talk centered on the importance of small gestures: "Never underestimate the power of your actions." He went on to tell the story of how Ryan had come to his rescue four years earlier after a bunch of bullies beat him up. He told of emptying his locker that afternoon and taking all of his books home. The reason: he was planning to commit suicide that weekend, and he didn't want his mother to have to return to school to clean out his things.

In a moving way, Kyle went on to say that his life turned around that day simply because someone had reached out in a desperate moment. "Ryan never knew it, but that day he saved my life." Then Kyle concluded, "I'm here to tell you that being a friend for someone is the best gift you can give."

ON THE RECORD

God Expects Your Best

I'd like to be remembered as one who always disciplined myself to give nothing less than my best, whether it be with family, business, government service, church, civic affairs, or athletics.

Chuck Cobb
Former U.S. ambassador to Iceland and business leader in Miami, Florida

What Kyle didn't realize is that Ryan may have gained even more from the befriending than Kyle himself did. When we reach out sacrificially to others, we are always the ones who gain the most. It is one of the greatest ways to grow spiritually.

One day a college physics professor gave his students a pop quiz. Well prepared, most of the class breezed through the exam — until they came to the last question: "Name the woman who cleans this classroom at night." Of course, no one knew the answer, but the message was clear: Be sensitive to the world around you; after all, we are all God's children.

I will never forget the first day Navy Lieutenant Jim Herzog walked into our midshipman class on navigation at Columbia University. He had just completed a three-year tour aboard an aircraft carrier and was now assigned as an assistant professor of naval science. He had never met any of us before that fall day, but he had spent the summer reviewing our military personnel files.

"Gentlemen," he said, "soon you will become naval officers, and this course in navigation is very important. But the first thing you must do is to know and respect those around you. Only then will you become a true leader." With that, Lieutenant Herzog went around the room, randomly pointing to each one of the forty students in his class and identifying each by name and hometown.

I would have followed this inspiring human being anywhere, anytime. With this simple gesture he had taught me the importance of reaching out to those around us and taking the time to know their interests, concerns, talents, and needs. Jim Herzog saw this as the means to becoming an effective Navy officer, but I see it as God's way of reflecting His love through what we do. It is called empowerment.

In your life you will meet many people. Some are powerful and famous. Others quietly do their work, unsung and unappreciated.

All deserve your attention and encouragement. And all around you are people with devastating problems: broken relationships, money fears, a marriage on the rocks, a kid on drugs, a parent dying of cancer. They are lonely beyond measure, and their life is adrift.

Yet most people won't tell you their hurts unless you know them well, and even then, many are unwilling to open up. That's why a smile, a warm hello, and a sincere indication that you care can be absolute lifesavers.

Often the most powerful gift you can give a friend or loved one is to pray on their behalf. Simply saying, "I am praying for you," lifts the spirits of believers and reminds the rest of the world that God is there to help.

Life will be much more exciting and rewarding when the best you have to offer is shared with others. God has given us powerful tools to use: praise, a warm smile, hope, concern, good examples, the comfort of His presence, and the promise of eternal life.

Nothing lifts your inner spirit more than this spirit of giving. Pat a person on the back or visit a friend in the hospital — and watch them smile. Buy a kid a baseball glove, and who's happier — the kid racing off to the playground, or the guy watching the kid run off with his new glove?

The old school of thought is that we ought to give to

ON THE RECORD

An Odd Number

A real Christian is an odd number:
Talks to someone he cannot see.
Expects to go to Heaven on the virtue of another.
Admits he is empty so he can be full.
Admits he is wrong so that he can be right.
Goes down in order to get up.
Is strongest when he is weakest.
Is richest when he is poorest.
Is happiest when he feels worst.
Dies so that he can live.
Gives away so that he can keep.
Sees the invisible, hears the inaudible, knows
that which passes all understanding.

A. W. Tozer

charity because it's right or because it makes good tax sense. The better way to think about generosity is to realize there's more in it for you than for the one who receives the gift. That is the mark of a caring Christian, who always adds newness to life while helping others discover the power of a loving God.

Nancy Atkinson learned that lesson in a powerful way. One day her daughter, Elaine, went off to school after giving her mom a kiss good-bye, as she did every day. But this day was special; it was Elaine's fourteenth birthday. What Elaine did not know is that her mother was preparing a very special present for her.

Five years earlier, Nancy had been diagnosed with terminal cancer, and now she was bedridden and unable to walk. But lately, with the help of neighbors, nurses, and medication, she had been practicing the painful movement of sitting up and standing alongside the bed. Her goal was to give her daughter a huge birthday hug when she came home from school.

ON THE RECORD

Feature Little Things

I truly care for the patients and individuals that I come into contact with.... I try to do the little things that help others cope with adversity — a friendly smile, directions when they are lost, a helpful hand or bit of advice.

Dr. Marcia Wright
USA Today **honoree,
Kansas City, Missouri**

The nurses were doubtful, but their patient was determined. She had every reason in the world to give up, but refused to do so. That afternoon when Elaine walked in the door, she found her mother sitting on the edge of the bed. As Elaine approached the bed, Nancy stood up and gave her daughter the most precious gift of a lifetime: a warm and tender stand-up hug.

For that precious moment Elaine forgot about the years of pain her mother had endured and how dark the future looked. It was a moment of pure joy. And that's the way her mother wanted it to be.

Nancy Atkinson was living out a miracle, thanks to the power of her inner spirit of determination.

Six months later, Nancy died. She wanted that birthday message to define her legacy. And it did.

Armed with her mom's heroic example, Elaine went on to earn honors in college and was selected by *USA Today* as one of the nation's outstanding young leaders in the newspaper's All-USA Academic All-Star award program. After obtaining her master's degree in public administration from the John F. Kennedy School of Government at Harvard University, Elaine got married, moved to Utah, and now specializes in community building and conflict resolution.

"My mother's unselfishness is a legacy I try to live up to each day," Elaine Atkinson Gause says. "I will never receive a more precious gift. I learned from her the importance of humility and need to give out as much love as you can. I also discovered the reality that you can even find success in failure."

Like Nancy Atkinson, most of us long to become the kind of people who not only uplift their own lives but also give hope to others. It is called radiating God's love no matter what the circumstance.

Each year *USA Today* honors about eighty top college student leaders for excellence in academics and community service. All have been empowered very early in their careers. Like Elaine Gause, they include some of America's best and brightest. After assuming major leadership roles in college, many past winners have subsequently moved ahead in serving those in need. They are committed to leveraging their talents and education to help solve problems around the world.

One honoree brought hands-on science projects to fifth graders, another worked with troubled teenagers in state custody, and another brought food and clothing to the homeless. Several honorees led projects dealing with AIDS, threats to the environment, and the work of medical missions in Third World countries. One sought to defend the rights of a forgotten native Indian tribe whose roots were in the very northeast corner of California. Another worked with the vision impaired, collecting eyeglasses and establishing vision-screening services in remote regions of the world.

Some mentored inner-city high school students, while others worked with the homeless, abused kids, and battered women. Still another worked as an election monitor in Kosovo's first national elections in modern times. Another started a huge community-based literacy program, and others volunteered to provide disaster relief.

Granted, these winners represent only the cream of the crop of their generation, but their unselfish service provides an important example for others to follow. Community service is important at all times, but especially in hard economic times and when governments from local to national face large budget deficits. We simply cannot expect government to solve every social need; community volunteers must help out. And these dynamic young people are leading the way.

Over and over the honorees have said that they feel it is their duty to serve. They value family and friends, but see community service as an essential responsibility. They are demanding good schools, safe neighborhoods, and leaders with character and integrity.

ON THE RECORD

Unconditional Love

I have drawn on an even greater love than that which I shared with my husband [Colonel Rick Husband, commander of space mission Columbia]. The unconditional love that comes from God who has been there in times I have wept and yelled as well as in times I have rested in Him. . . . That love is never-ending.

Evelyn Husband

They know there are no free rides in life. Facing a world of enormous change and turmoil, their generation believes that flexibility and self-reliance will be the keys to survival. They are not counting on Social Security or retirement benefits from their jobs. So they are working hard to assure their own futures while helping to meet the needs of the less fortunate. Their stories and comments on sharing with others give readers encouragement and hope.

There is a common thread to what they report: their lives are centered on *faith*, *family*, and *friends*. Those who had no family were uplifted by surrogate parents. Some were forced to find answers on their own. Nearly all were beneficiaries of the American Dream — arising from modest roots with a determination to come out on top.

As they shared their experiences and personal values through a special leadership survey conducted for this book, a common theme energed: that faith in God is central to their being, to their focus.

Jason Prince, a Davidson College graduate and *USA Today* honoree, puts it well: "In serving those in need, you possess the ability to not only touch the lives of others but to learn a great deal about yourself in the process." While in college, Jason took care of a professor's son who was recovering from leukemia. Later he served as a mentor for a mentally challenged high school student. This experience inspired him to create a program in which college students could mentor special-education secondary students. Those desperately in need of encouragement were around Jason, and he sought them out.

As the years go by, carving out time to help and uplift others can become increasingly difficult. Demands on your time are

Discovering His Direction

God has blessed us all. I live seeking His direction in my life and living expectantly in His loving grace.

Sharon McColl
San Diego, California

huge. There is work to do, bills to pay, and kids to raise. With such pressures, it is understandable that some people would tend to circle the wagons and take care of their own needs first. But God demands more from us.

A crisis occurs nearby and you need to step in. You move into another neighborhood or a new job, and right away someone nearby whom you hardly know becomes terminally ill. The son of a friend is killed in an auto accident. A person down the street or down the hall loses her job and the money is running out. And there you are, hardly acquainted with those involved, but vital to their needs. That's often the way it goes.

The bottom line: Get involved in good deeds — one person, one day at a time. God has empowered us for just such purposes.

That was the clear and persuasive message in a handwritten note I received from Allen Michalowski several years ago. In it he offered some thoughts on how to live true to the Word of God:

Uplifting God's Children

Speak to people. There is nothing so nice as a cheerful word or greeting.

Smile at people. It takes 72 muscles to frown, only 14 to smile.

Call people by name. The sweetest music to anyone's ears is the sound of their own name.

Be friendly and helpful. If you want friends, you must be one.

Be cordial. Speak and act as if everything you do is a joy to you.

Be genuinely interested in people. You can like almost everybody if you try.

Be generous with praise and cautious with criticism.

Be considerate of the feelings of others. There are usually three sides to a controversy: yours, the other person's, and the right side.

Be eager to lend a helping hand. Often it is appreciated more than you know. What counts most in life is what we do for others.

Have a good sense of humor, a huge dose of patience, and a dash of humility. This combination will open many doors, and the rewards will be enormous.

We all know people like Allen Michalowski, don't we? They are the ones who always manage a smile, even when they are hurting. They make a practice of focusing on others, not themselves. They ask how you are doing before you can find out what's up with them. They pass along compliments, spread cheer, and help others find some good news even when there is precious little of it around.

To me, unselfish people like that are unsung heroes in life. They are radiating God's purposes every day. They seek no credit nor expect it. They help others as both a natural and a personal obligation. Burned into their souls is a determination to help build a better, more caring world, one person at a time. What a great way to go through life!

As a newspaper publisher I tried to find stories about such people for my weekly column. It was a place in the newspaper where I could feature ordinary people who I thought were doing extraordinary things to help improve our community. Their wonderful examples of goodness to others served to uplift us all, especially when times were tough.

It is highly important to respect and honor good people around us. So often we are in such a rush in our daily routines that we become rude and uncaring and neglect the need to share with others.

At work there are literally dozens of ways for us to reflect our faith without wearing it on our sleeves or turning off those who might be seeking life's greater meaning. Our demeanor, our words — especially those carelessly spoken — are carefully scrutinized, especially by the cynics around us. Therefore we must never forget that our personal example can radiate the only Bible some people will ever see. In such circumstances we truly are God's ambassadors, as the apostle Paul reminds us in his letter to the Corinthians.

One of the first commitments I made as the new publisher of *The Miami Herald* was to meet all employees in person. At that time we had more than 3,500 full-time and part-time employees, spread over three shifts and writing stories, selling advertising, laying out pages, running the presses, and delivering some 450,000 newspapers to homes up and down the state. So to meet everyone was a formidable task, but an important one. Many of the sessions were held between midnight and dawn, especially at the distribution centers, where newspaper carriers met to assemble the newspaper sections and place them in plastic bags. It was my way of showing my concern for them and my appreciation for what they were doing. In the end, I hoped I was showing God's love through my demeanor.

At each employee meeting I invited questions, and on one occasion a hand popped up almost immediately. A man in the back of the room stood up

ON THE RECORD

Never Defeated

Whenever my sister or I expressed doubt in our abilities, our parents would remind us, "If you think you're beaten, you are. If you think you dare not, you don't. If you'd like to win but think you can't, it's almost a cinch you won't."

Jason Prince
Boise, Idaho

and said, "Sir, I didn't get your name. My boss ordered me to be here, but just what do you do around here anyway?" I have often reflected on that story, humorous at my expense, and wonder what my answer will be when God asks me, "Dick, just what did you do down there on earth anyway?" I hope I will have a good answer.

While in South Florida, I became good friends with Bill Marriott, who has been chief executive of Marriott International for more than thirty years. Bill is a person of great integrity who reflects his faith every day with his family and more than 125,000 staffers who work for his organization, which has consistently been named to *Fortune* magazine's list of most admired companies in America. The world knows that Bill Marriott is a man of God.

Bill spends huge amounts of his time simply walking around his hotels. He visits as many as two hundred a year. "You can tell by looking your people in the face whether they're happy. If they are not happy on the job, customers are not happy being with them. Keeping workers happy means not hiding in the office, but walking among the employees to look into their eyes and measure their mood."

Bill's hands-on management style is legendary, one that he sometimes reduces to six headlines:

The 6 most important words: I admit that I was wrong.
The 5 most important words: You did a great job.
The 4 most important words: What do you think?
The 3 most important words: Could you please?
The 2 most important words: Thank you.
The most important word: We
The least important word: I

If you think about it, each one of those principles is grounded in the Bible. I admire Bill because so many know that he lives out his faith in the real world every day — with integrity, humility, and concern for others. It is no surprise that Bill Marriott is one of the most respected business leaders in America. Marriott employees care about their organization because they are reminded constantly that their leader cares about them.

Most of our waking hours are spent at work. Our workplace is where we represent God and share the blessings He has given us. That is where we have the most contact with others. That is where our faith is challenged to express itself through kind words, a simple smile, a gesture of concern, or a humble deed.

Business leaders who are also Christians believe in the unlimited potential of each person in their organization. Such executives believe that we are all created in the image of God and that the success of each leader depends on the success of those around him or her.

Dealing with people at any level requires basic common sense. Reach out and show sincere concern for those around you. Show an interest in what they do. Find out what's bugging them. Take the time to discover their hurts and their dreams. These are some of the ways you can radiate God's love and serve His purpose.

FAITH KEEPERS

Who Needs Your Help?

- A single person looking for a healthy relationship.
- A clerk whose mother is dying of cancer and needs consoling.
- A friend whose marriage is falling apart and needs a sympathetic ear.
- A kid who desperately wants someone to look up to.
- An older person who wants to feel needed.
- A person who is terminally ill and needs prayer.
- A confused young adult who is struggling with life's priorities and meaning.

How to Share God's Blessings

- Feed the hungry and clothe the needy.
- Comfort the sick and dispirited.
- Be hospitable to those who know no one.
- Share God's love with the loveless.
- Visit those who are confined or disabled.
- Speak for those who cannot speak for themselves.
- Count your blessings and remind others of theirs.

Chapter 8

SERVE TOGETHER

GOD'S LOVE

"As I have loved you, so you must love one another."

John 13:34

MY MOST IMPORTANT RESPONSIBILITY

If our children had not grown up to be caring, responsible, independent adults, I would have felt that, whatever else I might have accomplished, I had failed in the most important responsibility God gives most of us the privilege of undertaking.

Former U.S. Senator Sam Nunn, Georgia

FAMILY HEROES

I have underlying respect for the broad-shouldered family man and woman who care more about their kids than themselves, and they are willing to make sacrifices so that their children can succeed.

Former astronaut Colonel Frank Borman, Las Cruces, New Mexico

LIFE'S ULTIMATE ANCHORS: FAITH, FAMILY, AND FRIENDS

At the end of life, you will never regret not having passed one more test, nor winning one more verdict, nor closing one more deal. You will regret time not spent with a husband, a child, a friend, or a parent.... When all the dust is settled and all the crowds are gone, the things that matter are faith, family, and friends.

Former First Lady Barbara Bush, Houston, Texas

One way our faith empowers us to make a difference in our world is how we function as families. We may not think of family as a way to demonstrate our faith, but consider this: If Christ's love doesn't make a difference in our marriages and family life, what does He have to offer the world? In other words, our families are really a microcosm of our faith. It is in the rough-and-tumble of being a family that we demonstrate how God works in the world. Yet we all know only too well that the institution of family in society today is in serious jeopardy. As Billy Graham once said, "This problem does not make screaming headlines, but like termites, it is eating away at the heart and core of our social and moral structure."

You are probably thinking, "I'll bet he has one of those perfect families where nothing ever goes wrong." I wish I could say that's true. But we're not perfect, and we would be the first to admit that. In fact, there is no such thing as a perfect family. Like you, we have had our moments of heartbreak and frustration and disappointment. When I say that we have a great opportunity to witness to God's love through our families, I don't mean we have to have the best-behaved or the best-looking or the best-educated kids. Too many Christian parents think that way and usually end up trying to create an image to cover up the real thing.

No, what I am talking about is doing our best as parents and family members to demonstrate unconditional love, especially when someone lets us down. Families will have conflicts. Kids will be kids. But one of the best ways to witness to the wonderful love

ON THE RECORD

Your Ministry

The Bible tells us that everyone in the family of God is a minister — just do not necessarily have to run a church.

Ken Blanchard
Author and management consultant

God has for us is to create an atmosphere of love and acceptance in our homes. It is called unconditional love.

This idea is what gives the parable of the prodigal son such a powerful message. The father in the story had every right to reject the son who squandered his life, but he threw him a party instead. It is that kind of love that appeals to the world, and through our family relationships we have a great opportunity to practice it.

Ideally, we plant this concept of love in our vision as we look forward to marriage. When Joan and I were dating, we talked at length about our goals and priorities. The subject always turned to family. How important is family to us? How committed were we to each other and to the rest of our family? How did we feel about having children and all the responsibilities of parenthood? These conversations were an amazing experience for both of us, because we were coming from opposite ends of the spectrum. Joan's parents shared a special closeness I could sense immediately, while my family had imploded, not once but several times. Joan knew the power of a loving family environment, and I knew it only through the huge void created while I was growing up. I saw that coming from a family devastated by divorce did not mean that I had lost the opportunity to create my own family centered on God's love and tenderness.

I can thank Joan for that. While putting up with my imperfections for four decades, she has enriched my understanding of the Word and of God's unconditional love and has been integral to every important thing I have done. My life would have little mean-

ON THE RECORD

Learning Ultimate Love

It's not so much what people say about you, it's what you have left behind. . . . When my three boys grow up, I want them to love their Lord and to love their wives.

David Robinson
U.S. Naval Academy graduate,
Olympic gold medalist, NBA star

ing without her. Her love has been patient and honest. She has brought out the best in me, has helped keep life in perspective, and has provided absolute candor when I have needed it most.

If you have not been focused on this kind of family environment, it's not too late to start. Plan a special "date" with the purpose of taking stock of how your family life reflects your faith. Are you pleased with the way you respond to conflict? When your kids and other close family members disappoint you, do you respond in a way that reflects God's love, or are you more likely to respond in anger? Be honest with each other, and show plenty of grace if either of you needs to change. Commit to helping each other and working together to develop a climate of love and understanding. Approach this as an adventure, not another list of "improvements" you need to work on. Regardless of what you face as a family, you can be a strong and memorable witness for Christ in the way you treat each other in the good times and the bad.

In our case, Joan has devoted her life to providing essential anchors for each of us in the family. Now, after all those years of challenging parenthood, we can savor the great joy that comes through the lives and experiences of our three grown children, their spouses, and our grandchildren. There is something very special about your children growing up, going off to college, finding challenging careers and meaningful lives, having families of their own — and then becoming mentors to *you*. Now they are encouragers to us, offering wise counsel that is both important and comforting. Once, when our kids were young, we sought to empower them. Now, as adults, they empower us. What a gift from our loving God!

ON THE RECORD

A Single Parent

My mom raised me as a single parent. She has always been there to encourage me and to help me through problems. Through her perseverance, I learned to remain strong in tough times.

**Justin Carroll
Wynne, Arkansas**

Sadly, not all couples stay married as long as we have been, yet half of all marriages actually *do* work. There is a huge world out there of caring and hardworking parents whose lives are centered on family, and they are willing to make the personal sacrifices essential to that commitment. They represent the best of a promising future. Pastor Greg Laurie, founder of Harvest Ministries, puts it best:

> Without hesitation, marriage lived out according to God's principles is the most fulfilling and wonderful thing that I know on this earth — next to salvation itself.

Family is where values are taught, where character is molded. It also is where most kids are introduced for the first time to a loving God. Parents teach their kids to pray, to believe in something greater than themselves, to appreciate their blessings. Families encourage and embrace, share and serve. Parents are sympathetic listeners when you desperately need to pour out your deepest hurts. And, just as important, they are the ones who will remind you when you are off course or have a dumb idea. They call it as they see it; that's what loving families are for.

If you are fortunate, you have been blessed by parents who have guided you every step of the way. In many cases today, that special care might have come from just one parent or a grandparent or even a sibling. Their love has helped you through disappointment and defeat.

ON THE RECORD

True Happiness

I've learned that if you pursue happiness, it will elude you. But if you focus on your family, the needs of others, your work, meeting new people, and doing the best you can, happiness will find you.

Unknown

They have been there to help you pick up the pieces in failure and to celebrate with you your victories. They help you sort out priorities and choices in life. They are always there, no matter what — in good times and bad. Involved and caring parents use their energies to inspire their children to do their best, work hard for good grades, and stretch to achieve their dreams. It takes a strong inner spirit to get them there.

Kids respond well when we tell them they are good. They want responsibility and need it. They should have chores. They must understand what is expected of them and strive to achieve it. It's as simple as that. In our household our children knew what their "job" was and that they were responsible for helping around the house, studying hard, completing their homework, getting good grades, and aspiring to achieve their full potential. Frankly, I don't recall hounding our gang to finish their homework or to study harder for exams. They did it because they knew it was their responsibility to do so.

It is natural to want to shelter our children from the hard lessons of life, but we can't and shouldn't. They grow from mistakes and failures. In many kids' sports today, every team member gets a trophy at the end of the season no matter how they perform. Unfortunately, life is not like that; there are winners and losers. Success takes sustained commitment and hard work. Hard work leads to achievement, and one small success inspires another. One small door of opportunity leads to another. A good grade in one subject inspires better grades in tougher courses. One teacher's praise builds confidence, while a coach's pep talk helps win the game. It is through this process that young people can prepare for the future, tap their potential, and build their dreams.

ON THE RECORD

Don't Miss the Boat

If you are living your life around a temporary role and allowing your treasure chest to remain barren ... then you are letting yourself be seduced by the culture and robbed of the true richness of your life — the deep and lasting satisfaction that only comes through family relationships.

Stephen Covey
The 7 Habits of Highly Effective Families

It is exhausting to think about those hectic years when, like millions of other mothers, Joan rushed in every direction for Little League baseball games, early morning swimming practice, soccer games, tennis lessons, water polo scrimmages, school plays and musicals, class field trips, art classes, and the like.

We struggled with homework and final exams and wrestled with term papers well into the night. Then came college entrance exams, a long wait for acceptances, and the emotional farewells outside their dormitories. Yet, before we knew it, they had advanced from little kids to teenagers to college graduates to parents in their own right to best friends, and we wouldn't for one minute trade those years of parenting.

When parents start early to nurture an understanding of God's ways, their kids have a huge head start in life. They arrive in school curious and smart beyond their years about the things around them. They understand how to treat others with kindness and respect. They have already learned about hard work and the need to do well.

Kids just know instinctively when their parents expect achievement and best effort. These expectations are passed along well before the first day of school. As I have watched my daughters and their husbands teach their children early on, I am amazed at what kids know these days, and I shudder at the challenges young parents face in raising children. Good kids today are kept busy with school, homework, and dozens of after-school activities. There never seems to be a spare moment for trouble or inattention.

Parents rush from one event to another, seven days a week. They worry about raising their families in this world full of violence, pornography, abuse, child molestation and abduction, alcohol and drugs. Competition for good grades and excellent schools is huge. Television is full of violence and sex as the media promote the glamour of Hollywood and the superficiality that goes with it. Nothing is hidden, and nothing can be pushed aside as too delicate to discuss.

In today's vernacular, moms and dads are referred to as "helicopter parents" as they hover protectively overhead. They feel they have no choice as they seek to provide stability and character in a confused and scary world.

A friend once gave us this checklist to help with parenting duties. Sometimes it helped us keep our sanity:

Have a sense of humor. You'll never survive parenthood without it.

Be honest and open. Kids will respect you for that.

Laugh even when the kids drive you nuts.

Support and encourage each other. It only feels as if it's you against the world.

Develop family traditions. The memories will carry you for a lifetime.

Take tons of pictures. Of all your "things" in life, nothing is more valuable.

Set aside family time. It's easy to let stupid things take precedence.

Plan family adventures. There's nothing like them.

Hug your kids every day — even when they are teenagers.

Demonstrate solid values by what you do, not by what you say.

Be confident, positive, and affirming.

Encourage your kids to have strong friendships.

Promote a passion for learning and a curiosity about life.

Talk openly about goals, priorities, and dreams.

Above all, thank God every day for the blessings around you.

Successful families don't just happen. They take huge amounts of work mixed with sacrifice and absolute commitment. Sure, parents fall short of the mark. There are always things we wish we had done differently. Pressures at work get in the way, family goals are abandoned or set aside, and we tend to believe that family priorities can be dealt with later — but that "later" never comes.

Kids need high expectations too. Joan and I were upset when a third grade teacher summarily told us that one of our children was never going to be any good in math. The third grade and written off in math? Give me a break! Such negative thinking can haunt people for life, denying them the opportunity to achieve their full potential.

If we tell our kids they will never get good grades, they will deliver Ds and Fs. Some parents accept mediocrity too easily. A child receives a failing grade, and the parents dismiss it casually even when they know it was caused by a careless lack of effort. If we let them off the hook when we know they can do better, we almost guarantee them lives of failure and disappointment. Without putting forth sustained effort when they are young, they never will get into college or get a good job. Worse yet, they will never reach their full potential, simply because they never really tried.

It is crucial that parents be encouragers to their children, because outside the home they are sure to face a full measure of hard knocks. The children also need to learn to be independent,

ON THE RECORD

Building a Lasting Legacy

My father always told me that, no matter what, it takes a lifetime to build a good, solid, honest reputation and all it takes is sixty seconds to ruin it.

Mike Fay
Businessman, Miami, Florida

relying on a quiet inner spirit to sustain them in good times and bad. Children need to believe that they can accomplish almost anything in life if they are willing to work hard for it. And they need to pray too. Only then will they become empowered by faith.

Author Robert Williams's advice in this regard is useful. He calls it "Gifts for Kids":

Raise your children to be strongly independent ... dependent on no one.
Raise them to question everything ... unceasingly.
Raise them to earn everything they want ... start early.
Raise them with all the love you can give ... all the time.
Raise them to understand that the only important things in life are faith, family, friends, fitness, and finance ... and in that order.

Let's face it: the track record of my generation is lousy. We've made it too easy for young people to get off track. They don't think it's a big deal to steal, cheat, or lie because they have seen so many others doing so. In these times of easy money and excessive wealth, they think that the "good life" is an entitlement. No wonder it's so tough to build that inner spirit centered on integrity and character. That's why it is so critical to be in a relationship with God and to see your work or study environment as a way to express His love and grace.

I want to encourage any of you who have had the misfortune of a divorce. Nearly 40 percent of all children live in homes without their father, and half of them have not seen their fathers in the past year. In 1960, 7 million children were living without their fathers; today the number exceeds 24 million.

When parents divorce, children feel rejected. They are six times more likely to grow up poor. They are much more prone to have emotional or behavioral problems, get pregnant outside of marriage, take drugs, or commit crimes. They become angry and depressed. Many turn to drugs or prostitution as a substitute for the love and attention they so desperately seek.

Divorced parents aren't immune from feelings of rejection, either. With so much emphasis on the family, it is easy for divorcees to feel as if they are second-class citizens. You need to remember that God is all about second chances. You may be struggling with the demands of a "blended family," but you can still demonstrate God's love through this situation. You can show the world there is something different about your family, despite the problems that come from divorce. In fact, you may be the very person others need to see, because so many divorced people are looking for examples of hope and healing.

No matter what our family's situation may be, we need to radiate God's love to those we care about. Peter Fonda, son of Hollywood's legendary Henry Fonda, grew up in a world that idolized his father, who unfortunately could not communicate with his own children. In a profile article in *Parade* magazine, Peter told how he desperately wanted his father's love, but Henry Fonda simply could not express it. The resulting void was devastating to Peter and continued to haunt him fifty years later.

Late in life, when frail and confined to a walker, Henry Fonda drew closer to his son. After one visit near the end, Henry said with tears, "I love you, Son." Peter hugged his father, got in the car, and wept like a baby. He had waited his entire life for those words. It

ON THE RECORD

My Best Friends

My mother and father were caring parents — always there when I needed them. I learned from them important values in life — honesty, hard work, and a good attitude. They are today my best friends.

Tracy Porter
Honey Creek, Iowa

is no accident that Peter Fonda has chosen to center his life on his own kids: "Every chance I get, I let my kids know I love them." That's not bad advice for any of us. "Just tell 'em you love 'em."

Jamie Foxx, the actor who portrayed Ray Charles in the popular movie about the singer's life, never had a relationship with his dad either. "I passed for more than a thousand yards, the first quarterback at my high school to do that," said Foxx, "but my father never came to my games. Even to this day — nothing — but that absence made me angry. It made me want to be something."

These experiences of Fonda and Foxx serve as profound and powerful reminders to all parents. It is a sad reality that there are people in this world, including parents, who love others but simply do not know how to show it.

By contrast, there is a very special group of women who volunteered their service in the pediatric ward at South Florida's huge public hospital in Miami. At the time, more than fifty "crack babies" were delivered every month. Most were abandoned at birth by addicted mothers who could hardly take care of themselves, much less the babies they had brought into the world. So from day one these tiny children — many born prematurely — never experienced a mother's touch. This catastrophic void was filled by this amazing group of surrogate mothers who came to the pediatric ward every day simply to hold and hug these tiny infants who so desperately needed love.

ON THE RECORD

Building Character
My parents focused on my developing a firm sense of right and wrong. Integrity is the foundation of an individual's character.

Keith Amos
USA Today **All-American winner, St. Louis, Missouri**

For children who have no family anchor, we need to create one. That's why, for the less fortunate, we must become an extended family, working through our churches. We need to volunteer at

United Way agencies whose purpose is to help needy children. Our local boys' and girls' clubs and dozens of other important community-based programs need our support. As Psalm 68:6 reminds us, "God sets the lonely in families."

In many cities, teachers become the only source children have for understanding values, morality, and character. Teachers in the classroom and coaches on the playing field become the only anchors some kids will ever have. If there are no parents around to nurture a young person's development, reinforcement from such substitute "families" becomes essential.

It will take a caring "extended family" community to help those without the stability of a family environment. As my former pastor, Dan Yeary, puts it,

> We live in an era of isolationism. We act like consumers who are entitled to privilege and that our particular "'kind" should be more privileged than others. We isolate, separate, and ultimately deprecate everyone we deem less important. We want our "community" to be exclusive, and we often ignore the value of the old, the young, and the other.

Some of the most needed mission work for our churches today is not halfway around the world; it is just down the street. The good news is that progress is being made. Churches sponsor programs to house inner-city kids, to feed the homeless, to build homes for the poor, and to adopt the abandoned. These efforts help keep kids off drugs, away from gangs, and out of prison. Above all, these efforts show them that others care and that there can be a future for them. Just because a person comes from a dysfunctional environment doesn't mean he or she needs to continue that downward spiral. Quite to the contrary. Sometimes those who have suffered the most from the absence of a stable family know the price that it extracts and become passionate advocates for stability and love — starting at home.

In the process of helping others, we need to make our own kids aware that community service is not only desirable but required.

Many young people today are deeply involved in neighborhood projects. Even elementary-age children are participating in closely supervised outreach efforts. Some teenagers, as they think about college choices, place heavy emphasis on universities that have a strong commitment to local public service. They want to advance their knowledge, of course, but want to make a difference too. It's God's mandate to us.

As one very unselfish friend once told me, "Everything I have is a gift from God, so it is my responsibility to give something back." What a great, faith-based approach to life. Said another way: It is my responsibility to be empowered by faith.

ON THE RECORD

Love All

My father died at age fifty. Even though he suffered physically throughout his entire life, he was always very positive and valued the challenge of a new day. These are values I try to apply each and every day: be positive, appreciate each day, love all.

Andy Hawes
Attorney, Boise, Idaho

Successful families don't just happen. They are the result of dedication, hard work, and a little luck. Beth Whiteman, another *USA Today* leadership honoree, put it this way:

> There is nothing like the sense of support that a family provides in good times and bad. And it's the simple things like eating dinner together, having a barbecue, and taking road trips that create a unique bond within a family.

The nightmarish experience of 9/11 and the events that followed jolted our sense of what's really important in life. Our first instinct was to embrace our family and close friends. We simply wanted them to know how much we loved them, how much we appreciated their closeness to us.

We can't solve all the problems around us, but we can impact those we love the most. That process must start in our own hearts, one person at a time. As the Reverend Jeffrey Metzer commented during a Promise Keepers conference for dads and their sons, "You change the man, you change the family. You change the family, you change the community. You change the community, you change the county ... the state ... the nation."

Yes, we are all in it together — friends and family — serving others by creating caring environments of comfort and reassurance. And it is a seven-day-a-week job, not just a task at church on Sunday.

FAITH KEEPERS

God's Gifts for Family and Friends

- The Gift of Listening

  But you must really listen — no interrupting, no daydreaming, no planning your response.

- The Gift of Affection

  Be generous with appropriate hugs, kisses, pats on the back, and handholds. Let these small actions demonstrate the love you have for family and friends.

- The Gift of Laughter

  Share articles and funny stories.

- The Gift of a Written Note

  A brief, handwritten note may be remembered for a lifetime. It may even change a life.

- The Gift of a Compliment

  It can make someone's day.

- The Gift of a Favor

  Every day go out of your way to do something kind.

- The Gift of Solitude

  There are times when it is important to be left alone. Be sensitive to those moments.

- The Gift of a Cheerful Disposition

  The easiest way to feel good is to extend a kind word to someone.

Compliments of Pinky Laffoon,
Saratoga, California

Chapter 9

SHARE YOUR STORY

PREACH THE GOOD NEWS

The Spirit of the Sovereign LORD is on me, because the LORD has anointed me to preach good news to the poor. He has sent me to bind up the brokenhearted, to proclaim freedom for the captives and release from darkness for the prisoners, to proclaim the year of the LORD'S favor.

Isaiah 61:1 – 2

THE MEDIA'S SAHARA

Religion is a Sahara of coverage because newsroom gatekeepers don't understand its centerpiece value to most Americans.

Rolfe Neill, former publisher, *Charlotte Observer*

JOURNALISM OF HOPE

The issue boils down to this: Whether we in the media are going to continue to practice the Old Journalism of Despair or a New Journalism of Hope.... Cynics make bad journalists. Cynical reporters are determined to find dirt under every carpet, whether it's there or not. That's unfair.

Al Neuharth, founding chairman and publisher, *USA Today*

In this era of instant global communication, we have incredible opportunities to spread the good news about our faith and how it impacts all that we do. The pervasiveness of the Internet is huge, with access to it anytime, anyplace, virtually free. No evening news commentator will stand in our way. No editor will filter what he or she thinks we should read. It's our call entirely.

What this means is that we have an extraordinary opportunity to share the power of our faith in ways we never dreamed possible. What an important time for us to spread the Word of God!

Many of you are uncomfortable explaining your faith to the secular world mostly because it involves opening your heart in very personal ways. It also takes preparation and thought to summarize what you believe for those around you. In the end, though, your story is important, so you must not hold back.

Those around you need — and deserve — to know what moves you, what drives your faith. They need to understand the centrality of a loving God and His wish for your life. All this is especially true in these turbulent times when so many are searching for life's meaning and purpose.

> ## ON THE RECORD
>
> **Journalists as Human Beings**
>
> *When I interview guests, I feel very comfortable in referring to the U.S.A. as "my country." Yes, we are journalists, but we are also Americans. . . . Journalists should not forget that they are human beings and citizens.*
>
> **Tim Russert**
> **Host of NBC's *Meet the Press***

Using the almost limitless impact of the Internet, you can arrange a Bible study program, pass along prayers to missionaries in far-off places, or distribute sermons or music or important commentaries to people anywhere in the world. Maybe you will never get a book published or give a sermon, but you can write your own story on the computer and transfer it, almost free of charge, to a compact disc.

You may never write an article for your local newspaper, but you can email a friend who needs your encouragement. Maybe you will never be asked on local television to talk about your faith, but you can share your personal testimony online. You can ask for prayers in the privacy of an Internet chat room or become an online missionary, using the Web (or better yet, creating your own website) to uplift those serving God elsewhere.

Churches and mission programs have become very effective in leveraging their websites to support their work. Churches offer live videocasts of their Sunday services. Others handle prayer requests and offer online access to Christian bookstores, music, and missions abroad. The Billy Graham Evangelistic Association has provided missionaries with laptop computers, spare batteries, and satellite phones to help support their important, very distant missions. Thanks to the Internet, those serving the Lord in the far reaches of the globe are able to receive immediate encouragement and prayer from churches and individuals who underwrite their mission.

ON THE RECORD

Gotcha Reporting

I don't like "gotcha" reporting. Confrontational interviewing may be good TV show business, but it often distorts the news.

Lee Hills
Former chairman and CEO,
Knight Newspapers

Several months ago Joan and I helped organize a new community church in the San Diego area. Through this experience — using the Internet as an important source of information and encouragement — we learned that nondenominational, community-based churches like this one are growing very fast. Several hundred potential members were linked by email almost overnight. Plans were made, online prayers were shared, ideas were offered, and within a matter of weeks the La Jolla Community Church

(LJCC) was established — all made possible on an efficient fast track because we were able to combine the power of God with the enormous capacity of the Internet.

In less than six months LJCC was in business with a senior pastor, a small staff and offices, and more than seven hundred members and regular guests, who support its needs and programs, all accessible online. Like thousands of churches across the country, this new church has a dynamic website serving as the hub for reaching others in the name of God: an online prayer ministry, copies of past sermons, access to members in small-group Bible study, missions programs abroad, and more.

Harvard Professor Samuel Huntington stated recently that Americans today may be more committed to their religious beliefs and Christian identity than at any time in United States history. For us that spells opportunity and needs that must be met. Take a look at these statistics reported through the highly respected Gallup Poll:

- More than 71 percent of all adult Americans believe religion is increasing its influence on American life.
- Over 90 percent of the American people believe in God.
- 46 percent consider themselves to be evangelists.
- 85 percent identify themselves as Christian.
- 65 percent claim membership in a church or synagogue.
- 40 percent attend church or synagogue at least weekly.
- 60 percent say that they pray daily and that prayer has a positive impact on national and world events.
- The sale of religious books — now exceeding $2 billion per year — is also at an all-time high.

Tens of thousands are meeting regularly for Bible study. This phenomenon of weekly small-group gatherings to share the Word of God is present in thousands of cities and towns across the country.

Faith among young people is especially strong. At hundreds of colleges and universities, prayer groups and religious studies are central to campus life. According to Gallup, 48 percent of all teenagers attended religious services in the past week; 51 percent consider themselves religious.

One in four Americans now use the Internet for religious information, with more than 3 million going online each day to find religious information.

Rick Warren's book *The Purpose Driven® Life* has now sold more copies in hardcover than any other book ever published with the exception of the Bible.

The bottom line: there is a huge upsurge in things spiritual across this diverse land, and we must contribute to it our own story — one person at a time. And that's where you come in.

For too long we have been conditioned to think that we must not talk about our religious beliefs for fear that we might offend someone. There are those who do not want to hear about your faith, perhaps because they are too uncertain about who they are. Others are experiencing emptiness in their lives or are confused but are not willing to open up and talk about it. Still others resent those who may be well intended but turn them off by "preaching" to them.

In this environment, the natural inclination is to do nothing when deep down we wish we could help. Sadly, living this delicate balancing act has caused us to "go underground" in many respects. We are afraid to share the excitement of our faith in God outside of the comfort of our church environment and Christian friends. But that should not be the case, especially during these perilous times.

We go to great pains to respect the rights of non-Christians, and in return we expect others to respect our right to believe as we do. But that does not mean we must be silent about our faith. We have rights too. The U.S. Constitution provides a clear separation of church and state, and we are free to believe or not to believe as we wish. At times we go too far in taking religion out of our secular surroundings.

One of the most difficult challenges I faced during my careers as a public servant and a newspaper publisher centered on how to balance my beliefs as a Christian with the demands of that "real world." Chances are, you struggle with this too. Sure, we live in a free country where religion should not be imposed or forced on anyone; yet we are also free to believe and practice our faith, a freedom sometimes forced into the back room of life.

ON THE RECORD

Infusing the Media with Human Warmth

What we need most of all in our profession is a generous spirit, infused with human warmth, as ready to see good as to suspect wrong, to find hope as well as cynicism.

Michael O'Neill
Former president, American Society of Newspaper Editors

In 2004 the World War II Memorial was dedicated on the National Mall in Washington. On one of the marble walls of that beautiful monument is a quote from the famous speech given by President Franklin Delano Roosevelt immediately after the Japanese attack on Pearl Harbor: "With confidence in our armed forces, with the unbounding determination of our people, we will gain the inevitable triumph." Unfortunately, the final phrase of that sentence has been omitted: "so help us God."

This, to me, is a disturbing image of the times in which we live. We can't even mention God for fear of offending someone. This timidity is indefensible and dangerous. How can we possibly deny the spiritual roots of our nation, starting with a Creator who blessed it all? America is overwhelmingly a spiritual nation.

We get married in churches or synagogues, return occasionally on religious holidays, ask a cleric or rabbi to officiate at funerals, and pray at public events.

I wrestled with this matter of balance during my years in the newspaper business. I am sure you do too. Yes, we must respect those of other faiths or no faith, but how can we — and why should we — avoid talking about the most powerful force in our lives?

The reality is that many today *do* publicly discuss their faith and dependence on God. And we must too.

There is an amusing aspect of television coverage of professional sports. You know the drill: a football player is seriously injured, and many of his teammates and coaches fall to their knees in prayer while he is taken away on a stretcher. A baseball player hits a game-winning home run and rounds the bases with his hand and index finger held high — not to boast that he is number one but as a salute to God. A bruising football game ends, and a sizeable number of players from the opposing teams meet in the end zone, join hands in prayer, and give thanks to God for His many blessings.

In these highly visible moments, the networks have no clue as to what to say when the athletes pray or salute God on national television. So the TV producers hastily switch to some inane beer commercial. So much for media commentary on the world of the faithful.

On any given weekend you will find ten or twenty pages of sports stories in your local newspaper but hardly a column or two about

---

ON THE RECORD

Out of Touch

The astonishing distrust of the media isn't rooted in inaccuracy or poor reportorial skills, but in the daily clash of worldviews between reporters and their readers. They simply do not share political, religious, or monetary values of the general population.

John Leo
Columnist, *U.S. News & World Report*

religion news. Overall, the media do a miserable job of covering the world of the faithful. I call it "The Greatest Story Too Seldom Told."

Now I realize that sports is almost a religion to many people, and I am as big a fan as the next guy, eager to get the paper and check the scores. So I am not asking the media to give as much coverage to religion as to sports. But why should there be such little coverage of something so important to so many people?

Did you know that in many cities, four times as many people participate in some form of religious service each week than watch all those high school, college, and professional games combined? Rolfe Neill, a long-time newspaper executive and former Knight Ridder colleague, is right: religion coverage is a Sahara, a "newsroom wasteland," as far as many editors and reporters are concerned. They simply don't understand it, choosing instead to brush it off as boring or non-newsworthy.

When people find out my background, they often ask in amazement, "You're a Christian and from the media? That's impossible." Ouch! Yet I can understand their frustration, because newspapers, newsmagazines, and TV networks by and large do a terrible job of covering religion in their markets. They are so concerned that it might offend those who have no faith at all that they choose to ignore the 90 percent who believe in God. And that's wrong. Dead wrong.

Now that I am out of the newspaper business, my friends and acquaintances are very candid in expressing their feelings about the media. Their distrust is deep and very troubling. Most are convinced that all media — print and electronic — are

ON THE RECORD

God Makes News Too

Religion is the greatest story ever missed. Why are people who identify God — not politics or human endeavor — as responsible for changing world events not taken seriously by the media?

Barbara Reynolds
USA Today

out to "do in" America, hell-bent on destroying reputations and institutions.

According to a recent Pew study, the media "makes news rather than just reporting it." The study found that only 35 percent of the public thinks that the media get their facts right, while 38 percent described the media as "immoral." John Leo, a columnist for *U.S. News & World Report*, asks, "Why does the news business keep hiring more and more people who disagree sharply with their customers, many of whom are already stampeding out the door?"

Democracy — including religious freedom — cannot survive without the free flow of information, good and bad, but is it asking too much that it be balanced? As Michael O'Neill, once one of America's leading editors, comments, "If we are always downbeat — if we exaggerate and dramatize the negatives in our society — we attack the optimism that has always been a wellspring of American progress."

Sometimes it seems that we work so hard to respect the rights of others who wander through life with no spiritual roots at all that we shut off the daily opportunities we have to reflect the love of the living God who is central to our faith.

ON THE RECORD

Warm and Caring

I want newspapers to be warm and caring and funny and insightful and human, not just honest and professional and informative. That subtracts nothing from their ability to tell hard truths.

Jim Batten
Former chairman and CEO, Knight Ridder, Inc.

What really is needed most of the time is an ability to strike a delicate balance. Our goal should be to reflect our faith in ways that attract those who are fearful or angry, cynical or hurting. This must be done, not in a false or manipulative way, but to show that we who are Christians are genuinely committed to making the world a better place. Is this a lofty goal? Of course!

With the proliferation of information sources such as the Internet and cable television, newspapers and TV networks are experiencing dramatic losses in circulation and viewership. Some major metropolitan dailies have lost as much as 6 percent of their readers in the past year alone; prime-time viewing on the three major networks has dropped 30 percent in the past ten years. If these media hope to regain public confidence, they simply cannot continue to ignore news that impacts the central core of life for millions of Americans.

There also is a widespread conviction that most of the media are far too liberal, that there is too little attention to balance in news coverage, and that the news is full of errors and taken out of context. I read four newspapers each morning and can point to examples of imbalance almost daily.

It is a cop-out for news executives to blame their problems on a general distrust of public institutions, as severe as that might be. Some newsrooms simply don't take enough time to stay in touch with their readers. To measure the pulse of their communities is hard work that requires a major, time-consuming outreach by news executives.

Not long ago, media mogul Rupert Murdoch spoke candidly on this point in a speech to editors. "Too often," Murdoch said, "the question we ask is 'Do we have the story?' rather than 'Does anyone want the story?'" Readers and viewers deserve relevant news — information that affects the priorities of their lives.

When the media have an opportunity to cover a truly newsworthy religious phenomenon, they often miss the core of the story, or they simply don't understand its significance at all. Take some of the coverage of Mel Gibson's powerful movie *The Passion of the Christ*, for example. Some critics kept searching for justification that it was anti-Semitic and, with their herd mentality, dozens of media "experts" beat that drum without the benefit of the facts. One particularly outspoken critic babbled on without ever having seen the movie. By contrast, *The Passion of the Christ* has become a film classic, one likely to be important and defining for generations to come.

When *USA Today* was launched by Gannett in 1986, its publisher, Al Neuharth, emphasized his belief that newspapers must offer readers a sense of hope. He said at that time, "It is the constant negative tone that is getting the public down on the press and paves the way for demagogues on the left and right to rally people against the press to further their own causes." His statement was right on target, and it disturbed many editors.

This was a concept totally alien to many hard-nosed newspeople who saw such uplifting efforts as nothing more than "cheerleading," and that was not in their job descriptions. What Al Neuharth said then had an important impact on me during my years at *The Miami Herald*, where we worked hard to attract readers in a highly divided community. One way was to triple religion coverage that included extensive profiles on people who were doing good things through their churches and synagogues. The readers loved it and told us so. Why not? South Florida was a dynamic region spiritually — one-third Catholic, one-third Protestant, and one-third Jewish. The news opportunities were almost limitless.

Too often the media act as if the story doesn't exist. That is why we must be prepared to tell the story ourselves. If church and faith are important to the majority in America, then they need to have prominent media coverage, don't they?

Today's digital mind-set has created a whole new set of expectations. Readers and viewers know what news they want, how they want to get it, and who they are willing to get it from. According to a recent Carnegie Corporation study, more than 44 percent of those surveyed are already using the Web as their primary source of news, while only 19 percent turn to newspapers. The message is, if the mainline media aren't doing their job, the public will turn to other information sources.

Now, what is your role in all this? As your local media work to discover what readers and viewers want and need to read or see, they need your help — and push — in identifying potential faith-based news stories and commentary in your city. Think about the wonderful God-loving people who represent the best of your neighborhood or town. The ones who are everywhere promoting safe neighborhoods, good schools, and ethical public service. The majority who work hard to make ends meet and raise good kids. These can become wonderful feature stories, and they reflect the soul of your community.

As you think about what you can do, keep in mind that no effort to spread the news about faith in America can succeed unless you are willing to tell your own story — one person, one moment at a time. And you are likely to be called into action when you least expect it.

All this takes personal preparation and practice. Write out a few headlines that describe your faith, and commit them to memory. Design whatever approach is comfortable for you. It can be difficult to say why you want to do all this in a brief, casual conversation with a friend who asks a question because he's curious about what moves you — but don't worry. Just consider it a wonderful door-opener, a privilege God has extended to you. Make your thoughts inspiring and nonconfrontational, and remind yourself that your task is simply to plant the seed.

You may not have an opportunity to pray in the end zone or tell the world about your faith on national television, but you can reflect God's love everywhere else with those around you day in and day out.

Just tell your story, and God will do the rest.

FAITH KEEPERS

Where Do We Turn?

- The modern attempt to exclude God from public life has gone too far. We're in danger of lapsing into moral and social chaos.... We've put our hopes in materialism and it's failed. We've put our hopes in technological progress and it has failed. We've put our hopes in freedom from moral absolutes and it has failed.... And we don't know which way to turn.

  Dr. Billy Graham

Anchoring Life's Underpinnings

- No piece of software, no server or search engine will offer you the irreplaceable rewards of a loving personal relationship, the strengths and comfort of a real community of shared values and common dreams, the moral underpinning of a life lived well, whatever the financial scorecard.

- It is not enough to wire the world if you short-circuit the soul. It is not enough to probe the hostile environments of distant galaxies if we fail to resolve the climate of mindless violence and racial hate here in the bosom of Mother Earth. It is not enough to identify the gene that predetermines the prospect of Alzheimer's disease if we go through the prime of life with a closed mind.

  Tom Brokaw
  Former NBC news anchor

Chapter 10

LIVE GOD'S PURPOSE

Do It Well

If it falls your lot to be a street sweeper, sweep streets like Michelangelo painted pictures, sweep streets like Beethoven composed music, sweep streets like Shakespeare wrote poetry. Sweep streets so well that all the hosts of heaven and earth will have to pause and say: Here lived a great street sweeper who swept his job well.

Dr. Martin Luther King

Radiating Your Faith through Quiet Example

My faith plays a big part in my life. And my faith is very personal. I pray for strength. I pray for wisdom. I pray for our troops in harm's way. I never want to impose my religion on anybody else. But when I make a decision, I stand on principle, and the principles derive from who I am.

President George W. Bush

Telling God's Story

The world desperately needs to hear and see the love of God. But how will it happen if not through people around the globe?

Pastor Skip Heitzig,
Ocean Hills Community Church,
San Juan Capistrano, California

Most of us will never be a street sweeper or the president of the United States, but we are all God's children, blessed with enormous potential. That is why it is such an inescapable responsibility to radiate God's love. As Skip Heitzig challenges us so poignantly, "If we don't tell God's story, who will?"

How about you? What is your purpose in life? How are you using God's gifts? How do you radiate His love? What about your most important priorities — faith, family, and friends? Do they matter — really matter? Are you empowered by faith?

These are profoundly important questions, and the answers you give now can inspire life-changing actions. No one is perfect. Each of us succumbs too often to other masters — money, power, superficiality, fame. So we need to change by adjusting our priorities such that we become empowered to serve God's purpose for us. And keep in mind that setting your purpose is an ongoing process. Rediscovering your God-given talents is not a one-time need; it's a recurring God-given opportunity.

ON THE RECORD

Put Your Trust in Him

If you want favor with both God and man, and a reputation for good judgment and common sense, then trust the Lord completely; don't ever trust yourself. In everything you do, put God first, and he will direct you and crown your efforts with success.

Proverbs 3:4-6 TLB

Several years ago my wife and I visited Magdeburg, Germany — a small town where Hitler made guidance devices for his V2 rockets during World War II. In 1944 this city was leveled by Allied air forces as they prepared to sweep across the region to liberate Berlin. Then, for almost fifty years during the Cold War, Magdeburg was ruled by Communist leaders. Finally, the Berlin Wall fell in 1991, and the region was free at last.

During our stay in this city, frozen in time by a half-century of Communism, we met an East German woman who was born in the late 1940s and knew only a life of repression. Almost in tears she told us, "I don't know who I am or what to believe. All my life I have been lied to by the Communists." Now she was starting her life over again, without much time to do so. How sad!

This woman's comment has stuck with me ever since. "I don't know who I am." Imagine that! We Americans — from birth — are free to select our own path, our own priorities, our own faith. On the other hand, we are also free to drift, to miss life's purpose, to deny the need for a loving God to guide and protect us. Like that woman raised under East German Communism, we desperately need to know who we are.

What are you doing with your life? What are your aims? As the old saying goes, if you aim at nothing, you are bound to hit it. But if you find and rediscover the unique purpose God has for your life, you will strike gold.

Life needs purpose — His purpose — and it involves serving others, all to the glory of our loving God.

From time to time we all need to take stock, even when life seems to be moving along just fine, thank-you. We can get rusty and lazy and take too much for granted. It is easy to procrastinate when changes are needed in everyday living, but when bad things happen, we have no choice but to adjust quickly. Perhaps it involves a personal crisis, a broken relationship, a failed marriage, or the death of a loved one. Maybe you have been laid off or laid up. Or you have just learned that the company you work for has been sold and soon you will be merged out of a job. All that is important seems up for grabs and you are forced to examine everything you do. Life can change on a dime, as 9/11 reminded us all too well.

You can almost hear God asking the tough questions: Who are you? Where are you headed? Is your life focused on My promise? Have you turned your worries over to Me — really turned them over? Perhaps God is telling you to slow down and redirect the priorities of your life.

If God is first, before your family and friends, if He takes precedent in everything you do, you will discover that your life has become empowered — empowered by faith.

When Joan and I lived in Madrid, we often discussed our personal priorities. Our lives were changing, if for no other reason than we had just become empty nesters. It was one of those important moments when we needed a fresh look. We were far from home and all that was familiar. We knew that we would eventually return to California to reunite with our family, so those months in Spain provided a perfect threshold for renewing our purpose. There we celebrated our thirtieth wedding anniversary, and our three children were either in college or graduated and working. We had completed four challenging career adventures in government and the newspaper business and had built close friendships stretching from Miami to Madrid, from San Diego to Washington. How blessed we were!

For a time — all too brief — we were ambassadors for our country, but soon all that would end. Before us would open yet another exciting chapter and with it perhaps the most promising time of service in Jesus' name. Joan's dream was to attend seminary to

ON THE RECORD

Duty, Honor, Country

Don't you ever, ever — no matter what the provocation or invitation — turn your back on your God, or your country, or that flag.

U.S. Air Force General Daniel "Chappie" James

advance her teaching skills, and I was committed to write a book on personal values. Once again we were at a crossroad, and we needed to sense God's plan for us.

Every day is a gift from our loving Lord. As the Bible tells us time and time again, we don't own anything — not our talents, our resources, nor even our lives. We simply are stewards of God's blessings for a brief time, and we are accountable to Him for those gifts and the ways we employ them.

While in Spain, we took two days off to fly to Turkey, specifically to visit Ephesus, a once-thriving city located on the eastern shore of the Mediterranean Sea. It was for the church there that Paul wrote his letter to the Ephesians, which for me is one of the most inspiring books of the New Testament.

At the time of Jesus, Ephesus was one of the largest cities in the Roman Empire and, as such, a major crossroad on the trade routes between east and west. It had beautiful marble buildings complete with plumbing and sewer lines. In its center were a beautiful library, elaborate fountains, public baths, and a spectacular amphitheater designed so that every spectator could hear the performers on the stage. Ephesus, however, was overrun by violence and sin. Christians there needed hope and encouragement, and Paul provided it — even when confined to a dark and dirty prison cell in far-off Rome.

Our walk down the marbled streets of this hallowed site was one of those magical moments when all our blessings seemed to come together in quiet reflection. We could almost feel the hand of the Lord that afternoon as Paul's words to the Ephesians came alive to us as never before:

[God] has showered down upon us the richness of his grace ...

He planned that we should spend these lives in helping others ...

He has made peace between Jews and you Gentiles by making us all one family ...

Be humble and gentle. Be patient with each other, making allowance for each other's faults ...

Remember, the Lord will pay you for each good thing you do, whether you are slave or free.

From Ephesians, TLB

It was as if God was setting us up for the time when we would leave Spain and return home. We had serious work to do: Concentrate on family. Be humble and gentle. Devote more times to helping others.

Paul reminds us that in our search for a faithful life, no task is too large or too small, nor is it too unimportant. Some can influence hundreds or thousands; others may touch only a few in an entire lifetime. I recall meeting two Methodist missionaries who had been in Spain more than thirty-five years and had brought a total of just thirty people to the Lord in all that time. They saw it as their calling and never measured their success by numbers alone.

ON THE RECORD

What Really Matters

Material possessions, winning scores, and great reputations are meaningless in the eyes of the Lord because He knows what we really are and that is all that matters.

John Wooden
Former UCLA basketball coach

No matter whether we are captains of industry or collectors of trash, mother or child, a janitor or the boss, we remain equal in God's eyes. Equal in His love. Equal in His work. And equal in the opportunity to reflect His grace.

Yes, we can turn the tide, just as Paul did with the people of Ephesus. Do we simply accept the things we don't like, or are we willing to work together to make the world a better place? Are we a herd of animals, or can we become a freedom-loving, peaceful civilization with a soul?

ON THE RECORD

Live Each Day to the Fullest

Dream as if you'll live forever.
Live as if you'll die today.

Eli Cryderman's high school class motto
(quoting actor James Dean)
Caledonia, Michigan

Not long ago, Ben Stein retired after writing a weekly column on Hollywood for many years. He had grown disgusted with the phony glitz of movie stars and other celebrities who are worshiped one day and forgotten the next. "I came to realize," Ben said in his final column, "that a life lived to help others is the only one that matters. It is my duty, in return for the lavish life God has devolved upon me, to help others He has placed in my path. This is my highest and best use as a human."

God uses all our experiences — good and bad — to help mold who we are. Facing us out there are several paths, some right and some wrong. Each decision reflects how central a person's faith is. Some choose wisely and succeed. Others choose wrongly. They stumble, embarrass themselves, and hurt others. Their lives center on bad attitudes, complaints, criticism, cynicism, anger, failure, and frustration. They have worshiped the god of money and fame and then wonder how they could have wasted so many of God's precious days. Affluence often makes people forget who they are. Trappist monk Thomas Merton put it powerfully:

The most dangerous man in the world is the contemplative who is guided by nobody. He trusts his own visions.... He identifies the will of God with anything that makes him feel ... a big, warm sweet interior glow. The sweeter and warmer the feeling, the more he is convinced of his own infallibility.

Faithful people reflect praise, hope, and concern for others. They see this calling as a privilege, not a chore. Through our loving God we can always find hope, purpose, love, acceptance, courage, forgiveness, and comfort.

During my forty-year career in the newspaper business and government, I met hundreds of dedicated public servants who have made huge sacrifices to serve their country. Near to the top of my list of such people is former U.S. Senator Sam Nunn, a strong Christian leader who was beloved and respected on both sides of the aisle. I first met Sam when he was a state legislator and I was working for Mel Laird in the Pentagon. I greatly admired this good and unselfish man who radiates God's love in everything he does.

A lifelong Democrat from Georgia, Sam worked tirelessly on matters of foreign policy and national defense. For years he served as a talented and persuasive congressional leader and chairman of the Senate Armed Services Committee, but he had little patience for the negative and cynical campaign practices that consumed Washington. "Too often," he said, "the common sense of elected

ON THE RECORD

Our Challenge

The world knows a lot about Jesus, but do they know him? It is for the churches to seize this moment, to take the vague spirituality of the day and turn it into a faith that is solid and transformative.... Churches have neglected what they should be all about, and that's discipleship.... People look at churches and they don't see lives being changed. The core is getting mushy.... Anything that doesn't lead to Jesus should be cast off.

George Gallup Jr.
Public opinion researcher

officials is drowned out by the extremes of both parties who are usually wrong but never in doubt."

Everyone who knows Sam admires his personal character and impeccable integrity. Despite long hours on the Hill, Sam always made time for his family, especially during his daughters' growing-up years. "I tried always to be there when they had a game or school event that was important to them, and to actively share in their good times as well as their problems."

Sadly, Sam became increasingly frustrated with unnecessary divisiveness in Washington; for him politics wasn't fun anymore. So in 1995, after twenty-four years in the Senate, he shocked his colleagues by announcing his retirement at age fifty-seven. It was a huge loss for the nation. The decision to leave disappointed his friends on Capitol Hill, but his family was relieved. They wanted more of him. Walking away from such responsibility and power took courage, but he had his priorities in focus. Now Sam heads the Nuclear Threat Initiative, which is dedicated to reducing global threats from nuclear, biological, and chemical weapons.

Through Sam Nunn's unselfish service we learn that legacies are made out of a lifetime of service to others, not superficial adulation, huge fortunes, glitz, or fleeting fame. At his core he is a man of God, and he never lost sight of his Christian roots: "My father and mother lived their Christian faith. They always tithed, always went to church, and always took responsibility for doing their part." What does Sam consider his most important accomplishment

ON THE RECORD

The Final Legacy

Christians affirm that God, the all-powerful Creator of the universe, became a man in the person of Jesus Christ. He taught that God is love and that He is willing to forgive us when we commit our lives to Him. He offered us hope of an eternal heaven. I believe that He is the answer to every individual's search for meaning.

Dr. Billy Graham

during those Washington years? "Keeping my family together and helping my wife, Colleen, raise two wonderful children....
I believe that if America is to remain the greatest nation on earth, we must put our children first."

Several years ago Joan was invited to lead Bible studies for a group of women, some of whom she hardly knew. Many were not regular church-goers, and she had no idea whether or nor the Word of God was impacting their lives. One day, after returning from a long trip in Europe, Joan received a message from the husband of a member of that group. His wife had died suddenly, and he wanted Joan to deliver the eulogy. This widower told Joan that her teaching had made a huge difference in his wife's life — in his view, changing it forever. Joan had empowered this person's wife with faith. What a gift — and just in time. Joan's experience is a powerful reminder that we never know how or when the radiating power of God's love through us will take hold and change someone's life.

The only way I know to take on the Lord's work is to do so one task, one day at a time. My pastor in Miami, Dan Yeary, tells us how to do it. Perhaps his advice will be useful to you:

> Forget what you have done for other people, and remember what other people have done for you.
> Ignore what the world owes you, and think of what you owe the world.
> Put your rights in the background, your duties in the middle distance, and your chances to do a little more than your duty in the foreground.

See that your fellow men and women are just as real as you are, and truly try to look behind their faces to discover their hearts.

Stoop down and consider the needs and desires of little children.

Remember the weakness and loneliness of people who are growing old.

Stop asking how much your friends love you and ask yourself whether you love them enough.

Bear in mind the things that other people have to bear in their hearts.

Trim your light so that it will have more light and less smoke, then carry it in front so that your shadow will fall behind you.

Believe that love is the strongest thing in the world — stronger than hate, stronger than evil, stronger than death.

Envision a brighter future for yourself — and it likely will happen.

Never forget the blessings of each day.

Reach out and encourage a friend — or a stranger.

Express gratitude to someone who has helped you.

Read something uplifting.

Laugh about funny things and laugh at yourself. Nothing overwhelms failure or disappointments better or faster.

Don't go to bed without clearing up misunderstandings with those you love.

Discipline yourself to steer away from negative beliefs you may have.

Tell your family you love them.

Tell a friend how much they mean to you.

Make plans for tomorrow.

I hope that you come away from this book struck by the awesome privilege of your life. Perhaps you will have a renewed sense of the hand of God in your journey. Maybe you will find opportunities for humble service in His name, knowing that the responsibility to radiate God's love never ends.

God's call for us is clear: equip, enlarge, enable, encourage, prepare, pray, renew. Each task demands action. The Lord does not reward those who are far too comfortable, far too complacent. George Bernard Shaw expressed it persuasively:

> I want to be thoroughly used up when I die, for the harder I work, the more I live. Life ... is sort of a splendid torch which I have got hold of for a moment, and I want to make it burn as brightly as possible before I hand it off to future generations.

Despite the trauma of 9/11, we seem to have put faith in God aside once again. Life has been good, jobs plentiful, the economy booming. Our churches are not as full, and we find resentment toward anyone — including the president of the United States — who talks openly about the power of prayer and how faith is central to their lives. We cannot allow that.

Most of us want to aspire to something greater than ourselves. We want purpose, and we thrive on renewal. In the end, living a life of consequence — God's consequence — is all about "doing the right thing," no matter what. Don't worry about popularity. Ignore those who envy your accomplishments and refuse to praise your efforts. Don't be concerned if the entire world forgets all the good things you have done. All that matters is knowing that you did your best, and got it right with the Lord.

ON THE RECORD

God's Love

My main desire in life is to reflect God's love in my life.

Ranjan Marwah
International business executive in Hong Kong

It is said that one day St. Francis of Assisi invited one of his students, Bernard, to leave the monastery and go with him into the nearby village to "proclaim the Gospel." Brother Bernard was prepared to hear yet another inspiring sermon from his revered teacher, whose witness and testimony had led him to Lord.

As they walked about town, Francis was friendly to the shopkeepers, greeting and talking with them and offering compassion along the way. Soon the duo returned to the monastery, but Bernard was disappointed. "Francis," he said, "I thought you were going to preach, but I did not hear any sermon." Francis, with classic modesty, responded, "Proclaim the Gospel at all times.... And, if necessary, use words.... It is no use walking anywhere to preach unless our walking is our preaching."

St. Francis said it all: *Our walking is our preaching.* What a powerful message for each of us. Put another way, we need to remember that God has blessed us so that we can bless others. This means we must appreciate and experience God's love every day in every way, and then reflect that love in all we do. That is how we can rediscover His ultimate empowerment.

Empowerment Requires ...

- Courage to do the right thing.
- Grace reflecting kindness and courtesy in dealing with others.
- Inner strength by relying on God to empower you.
- Doing your best. Striving for excellence.
- Being a truthful witness, giving honest testimony.
- Being kind and compassionate to others, including those you don't know or don't like.
- Seeing your work as a ministry, a mission.
- Seeing your work as a way to show your love for God.
- Stopping to say thanks to others and uplifting what they do.
- Giving thanks to God, especially when everything is going your way.

AFTERWORD

I hope this book will encourage you to live your faith effectively and humbly in a troubled and torn world. It is intended to be a message of encouragement and hope at a time when we seem to be facing a long stretch of uncertainty and crisis.

Empowered by Faith includes some wonderful on-the-record thoughts from people I respect; some names are undoubtedly familiar to you. I encourage you to share those quotes with friends. Copy your favorites and paste them on your computer screen or on the bathroom mirror or refrigerator door. Email them to friends. Put them on your website. The format of the On the Record and Faith Keepers features are designed for that purpose.

If you find this book useful to you, share copies with friends. Use it as the basis for discussion group study. Maybe the thoughts and ideas here will offer hope to others at the very moment they need it most. You never know when you might impact others in life-changing ways. That's God's purpose for you. As we are so often reminded, for many around us we are the only Bible they will ever know.

As a starter, take a few minutes to reflect on how this book has touched your life. How strong is your faith? How are you reflecting it in all that you do? What changes do you need to make in your life? Then take a few minutes to grade yourself, using the following Faith Survey. This survey is not intended to be scientific or all-inclusive but rather a tool to help bring focus to life's priorities.

If you rank high, *Empowered by Faith* will reinforce the key faith-filled motivators of your life. On the other hand, if you score lower, you now have some ideas for moving forward in your commitment to experience God's love every day.

Faith Survey

How Much Do You Radiate God's Love and Grace?
Rank each statement on a scale of 1 to 5, with 5 meaning "strongly agree."

I regularly count my blessings	1	2	3	4	5
I make changes easily	1	2	3	4	5
My family life is strong	1	2	3	4	5
The Lord is central to my life	1	2	3	4	5
I share my faith with others	1	2	3	4	5
I am an important mentor to others	1	2	3	4	5
I am cheerful in spite of circumstances	1	2	3	4	5
I go out of my way to help others	1	2	3	4	5
My faith in God is strong	1	2	3	4	5
I am willing to stand up for what I believe	1	2	3	4	5
I read the Bible and take time to reflect	1	2	3	4	5
I share my goals and dreams with those I love	1	2	3	4	5
I have a clear sense of where I am going in life	1	2	3	4	5
I have few regrets about what might have been	1	2	3	4	5
I am willing to admit my weaknesses	1	2	3	4	5
I do not fear failure	1	2	3	4	5
I pray daily	1	2	3	4	5
I do not get discouraged easily	1	2	3	4	5
I am optimistic about the future	1	2	3	4	5
The priorities for my life are in balance	1	2	3	4	5

Total _____

How Did You Score?

91 – 100 points	Your faith is solid
81 – 90	Your inner strengths need fine tuning
71 – 80	You are more discouraged than you need to be
60 – 70	You are in a rut, headed for trouble
Below 60	You need a faith lift!

GOD'S EMPOWERMENT

Included in this book are some special references from the Bible. Each is designed to help empower you with the Word of the Lord.

As you reflect on how *Empowered by Faith* might strengthen your life, take time to reread these quotes and consider how they might help inspire new ways to experience God's love each day.

TEACH

"All authority in heaven and on earth has been given to me. Therefore go and make disciples of all nations." (Matthew 28:18–19)

SHINE

Do everything without complaining or arguing, so that you may become blameless and pure, children of God without fault in a crooked and depraved generation, in which you shine like stars. (Philippians 2:14–15)

BE THANKFUL

Be cheerful no matter what; pray all the time, thank God no matter what happens. (1 Thessalonians 5:16–18 The Message)

TRUST GOD

Walk by faith, not by sight. (2 Corinthians 5:7 KJV)

PERSEVERE

Blessed is the man who perseveres under trial, because when he has stood the test, he will receive the crown of life that God has promised to those who love him. (James 1:12)

DO GOOD THINGS

For we are God's workmanship, created in Christ Jesus to do good works, which God prepared in advance for us to do. (Ephesians 2:10)

FOCUS ON HIM

Commit to the Lord whatever you do, and your plans will succeed. (Proverbs 16:3)

REFLECT GOD'S WILL

This is the wonderful message he has given us to tell others. We are Christ's ambassadors, and God is using us to speak to you. (2 Corinthians 5:19–20 NLT)

STAY ON COURSE

"What good is it for a man to gain the whole world, yet forfeit his soul?" (Mark 8:36)

LOVE WHAT YOU DO

There is nothing better for a man than to enjoy his work. (Ecclesiastes 3:22)

BE STRONG

"So keep up your courage, men, for I have faith in God." (Acts 27:25)

BE ENTHUSASTIC

Whatever you do, work at it with all your heart, as working for the Lord, not for men. (Colossians 3:23)

BE PREPARED

Prepare God's people for works of service. (Ephesians 4:12)

BE COMFORTED

What a wonderful God we have — he is the Father of our Lord Jesus Christ, the source of every mercy, and the one who so wonderfully comforts and strengthens us in our hardships and trials. And why does he do this? So that when others are troubled, needing our sympathy and encouragement, we can pass on to them this same help and comfort God has given us. (2 Corinthians 1:3–4 TLB)

FIND STRENGTH

When I am weak, then I am strong. (2 Corinthians 12:10)

LOVE THE LORD

And we know that in all things God works for the good of those who love him, who have been called according to his purpose. (Romans 8:28)

FIND HOPE

We also rejoice in our sufferings, because we know that suffering produces perseverance; perseverance, character; character, hope. And hope does not disappoint us, because God has poured out his love into our hearts by the Holy Spirit, whom he has given us. (Romans 5:3–5)

NEVER GIVE UP

Blessed is the man who perseveres under trial, because when he has stood the test, he will receive the crown of life that God has promised to those who love him. (James 1:12)

FINISH THE RACE

Let us run with patience the race that is set before us,

Looking unto Jesus the author and finisher of our faith. (Hebrews 12:1 KJV)

ENCOURAGE OTHERS

Do not let any unwholesome talk come out of your mouths, but only what is helpful for building others up according to their needs. (Ephesians 4:29)

FIND HIS PEACE

God is our refuge and strength,
an ever-present help in trouble.
Therefore we will not fear, though the earth give way
and the mountains fall into the heart of the sea....
Be still, and know that I am God. (Psalm 46:1–2, 10)

TURN YOUR TROUBLES OVER TO HIM

"Come to me, all you who are weary and burdened, and I will give you rest." (Matthew 11:28)

FIND THE GOOD IN LIFE

Live such good lives among the pagans that, though they accuse you of doing wrong, they may see your good deeds and glorify God on the day he visits us. (1 Peter 2:12)

BE HUMBLE

Do nothing out of selfish ambition or vain conceit, but in humility consider others better than yourselves. (Philippians 2:3)

LOVE OTHERS

"As I have loved you, so may you love one another." (John 13:34)

SHARE THE GOOD NEWS

The Spirit of the Sovereign LORD is on me, because the LORD has anointed me to preach good news to the poor. He has sent me to bind up the brokenhearted, to proclaim freedom for all captives and release from darkness the prisoners, to proclaim the year of the Lord's favor. (Isaiah 61:1–2)

LIVE A LIFE OF SERVICE

[God] has showered down upon us the richness of his grace...

He planned that we should spend these lives in helping others...

He has made peace between Jews and you Gentiles by making us all one family...

Be humble and gentle. Be patient with each other, making allowance for each other's faults...

Remember, the Lord will pay you for each good thing you do, whether you are slave or free. (From Ephesians, TLB)

TRUST THE LORD

If you want favor with both God and man, and a reputation for good judgment and common sense, then trust the Lord completely; don't ever trust yourself. In everything you do, put God first, and he will direct you and crown your efforts with success. (Proverbs 3:4–6 TLB)

ACKNOWLEDGMENTS

Writing a book, believe it or not, can be a painful process, especially for a type-A, high-intensity person like me. Let me be honest: The discipline of spending dozens of hours over many months in front of a computer screen behind closed office doors is not in my natural makeup. So this project took cajoling and prodding to get the job done. And that credit goes in important and much appreciated ways to Zondervan's associate publisher, Lyn Cryderman, who edited my first book, *Finish Strong*.

Lyn is a person of enormous writing talent, strong in his faith and dedicated to the mission of Zondervan that continues to serve the Christian and secular marketplace with inspiring impact. I now have worked with Lyn over the course of ten years and am grateful for his wise counsel. He is a dedicated and gracious servant of God.

It is no exaggeration to say that *Empowered by Faith* would not have seen the light of day without the continuous encouragement of my son, Chris Capen, who is a publisher of high-quality, four-color coffee table and corporate books. Chris knew what was on my heart to share, and he urged me to express it even when many distractions stood in the way, some of my own making.

Alongside Chris was my wife, Joan, who is convinced that writing books is a self-imposed torture I should experience only once in a lifetime — and here I was at it again. In her quiet and faith-filled ways she has influenced, far beyond measure, most of what

I have shared here. Above all, she helped me respect the fine line between being a writer, where my talents are modest, and a Christian, where I have so much to learn.

Writing this book took so long that most of my family, and virtually all of my friends, stopped asking when it would be published. They had heard every excuse imaginable and were convinced that the project had died long ago. Even so I thank them for the positive influences they have had on many of the thoughts expressed here. As for the book's imperfections, I take full responsibility.

Neither *Finish Strong* nor *Empowered by Faith* would have been possible without the wonderful encouragement and assistance I have received not only from Lyn Cryderman but also from so many of his key associates at Zondervan. I thank them for their confidence in me. I am grateful to Jim Ruark, who edited each chapter of this book with great sensitivity and professionalism, and Scott Heagle, who led efforts to introduce *Empowered by Faith* to the Christian and secular marketplace. I especially appreciate the unsung work of Joyce Ondersma and Jackie Aldridge, who head up Author Care services at Zondervan. These wonderful women have worked with me for over ten years in the distribution and marketing of my books.

I am enormously grateful for the more than 2,000 letters and emails I received from readers of *Finish Strong*. Their input was critical to this book as well. Also helping me in organizing the leadership survey results was John T. Tanner.

Special thanks go to my tennis friends, who have kept me humble on the tennis court during this project: Alan Balfour, Henry Ingersall, Judge Dave Moon, Steve Flynn, John C. Tanner, Tom Hansch, Jeff Nelson, and Jim Long. They will discover that during our mortal combat and controversial line calls, I was test-marketing some of the sage advice offered here.

In recent months Joan and I have been involved with a wonderful group of dedicated Christians who have organized a new nondenominational church, La Jolla Community Church (LJCC). It was an inspiring backdrop for completing this book, because in all our years of churchgoing we have never been around so many dedicated, faith-filled people who are so unselfishly serving the Lord. In a matter of months more than seven hundred people have joined to support LJCC. With the Reverend Steve Murray as our talented senior pastor and gifted preacher, a wonderful group of lay leaders, led by David Ruyle, has found new facilities, hired two pastors, opened church offices, launched strong music and youth programs, started several missionary efforts, and raised the funds to support it all.

In the end, my passion for writing this book centered on one simple reality: 9/11 changed everything for the rest of our lifetime. More than ever, I have felt that we need strong faith in God and the encouragement to radiate His love in every aspect of our lives. If this book contributes to that reality, *Empowered by Faith* has met its goal.

NAME INDEX

ABOUT THE AUTHOR

Dick Capen's career represents a unique blend of diplomacy and newspaper publishing. Known for his commitment to personal values and a positive approach to life, he has been a nationally recognized columnist, author, and speaker on contemporary trends in America.

Capen is the author of *Finish Strong*, which focuses on how to balance career with personal priorities and key values essential to a meaningful life.

For more than thirteen years the author served as a director and senior executive at Knight Ridder, Inc., one of the country's most respected media companies. For seven of those years, Capen was chairman and publisher of Knight Ridder's flagship newspaper, *The Miami Herald*. The newspaper received five Pulitzer prizes during his stewardship. Conversant in Spanish, Capen led efforts in 1985 to start *El Nuevo Herald*, which is now the largest and most successful Spanish language daily in the United States.

During his years at the the *Herald*, Dick Capen wrote a Sunday column that was widely read in both English and Spanish. From 1989 to 1991 he served as Knight Ridder's vice chairman.

Capen interrupted his newspaper career twice for tours in federal government. His first appointment was in 1968 in the Department of Defense, where he served as Deputy Assistant Secretary of Defense and Assistant to the Secretary for Legislative Affairs. In 1971 he received the department's highest civilian decoration — the

Distinguished Service Medal — for his leadership on prisoner-of-war matters and congressional liaison.

In 1992–93 Capen served as U.S. Ambassador to Spain, where he led efforts to expand business opportunities and educational exchanges. He also served as chairman of the U.S. Delegation to the 1992 Olympics in Barcelona. While serving as ambassador, Dick visited more than sixty-five cities in all seventeen autonomous regions of Spain.

In 1993 Dick Capen established the Ambassador's Award for Exceptional Leadership. The recognition is given each year to outstanding graduating high school students in Spain as an encouragement for them to study in the United States. More than seventy-five awards have been presented to date.

In 1991 Capen left the newspaper business so that he could devote more time to being an author and speaker on personal values essential to life. He serves as an independent director of Carnival Corporation and twelve of the American Funds. He also is a director of the Billy Graham Evangelistic Association.

Born in Connecticut, Dick Capen is a graduate of Columbia University, which he attended on a Navy ROTC scholarship. He and his wife, Joan, who holds a master's degree in theology from the Westminster Theological Seminary, have three grown children and four grandchildren. They live in Rancho Santa Fe, California.

Contact: 858-756-9989 or RGCapen@aol.com
Box 2494, Rancho Santa Fe, CA 92067

We want to hear from you. Please send your comments about this book to us in care of zreview@zondervan.com. Thank you.

ZONDERVAN®

GRAND RAPIDS, MICHIGAN 49530 USA

ZONDERVAN.COM/
AUTHOR**TRACKER**